Global Winners

74 Learning Activities for Inside and Outside the Classroom

Jan Drum, Steve Hughes, and George Otero

Global Winners

74 Learning Activities for Inside and Outside the Classroom

Jan Drum, Steve Hughes, and George Otero

Intercultural Press, Inc.

For information, contact:
Intercultural Press, Inc.
P.O. Box 700
Yarmouth, Maine 04096 USA
207-846-5168

Book design and production by Patty J. Topel
Cover design by Patty J. Topel

Printed in the United States of America

00 99 98 97   2 3 4 5

Library of Congress Cataloging-in-Publication Data

Drum, Jan.
    Global Winners: 74 Learning activities for inside and outside the classroom / Jan Drum, Steve Hughes, and George Otero.
       p. cm.
     Includes bibliographical references (p.   )
     ISBN 1-877864-18-8
  1. International education—United States. 2. International education—United States—Activity programs. I. Hughes, Steve. II. Otero, George G. III. Title.

LB1099.3.D78   1994
370.11'5—dc00   94-1404
                                   CIP

Acknowledgments

The activities in this book evolved from years of work with hundreds of students and colleagues. We have tried to credit specific individual contributions whenever possible. Beyond these individual credits, we want to thank those unnamed students and colleagues who have joined in our play, challenged us, and generously shared their wisdom and creativity. We appreciate also our colleagues at Intercultural Press, especially David Hoopes and Toby Frank. Finally we offer thanks and love to our families who supported this transcontinental writing project.

Dedication

In the human realm, we dedicate this work to our dear friend Bob
Freeman. In the realm of the mysterious, we are grateful for the
gift of Taos Mountain.

Table of Contents

x

xi

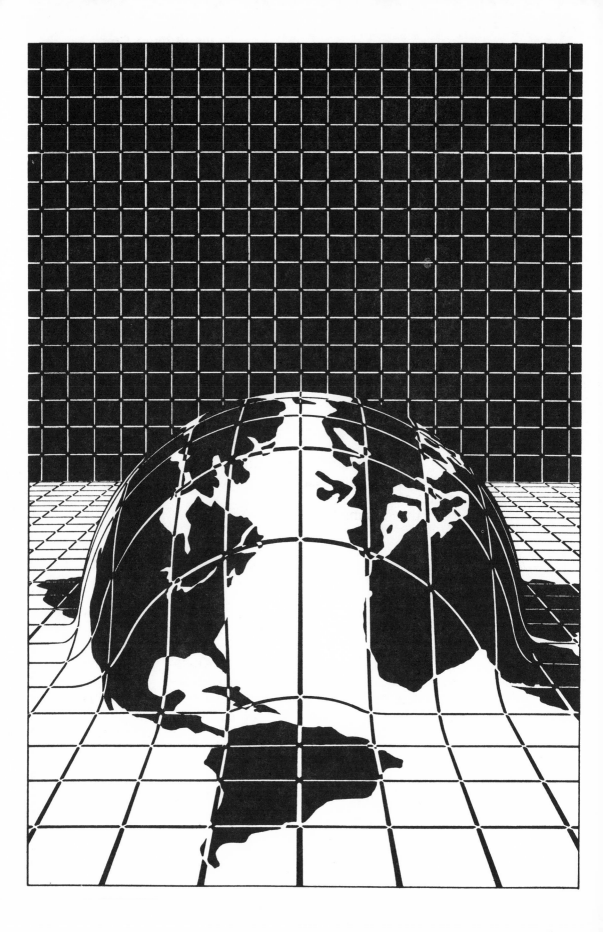

INTRODUCTION: THE IDEA OF GLOBAL LEARNING

In 1987, a teacher in an alternative school in Las Cruces, New Mexico, asked her students what five topics interested them the most at that moment. They said:

—nuclear waste disposal in southern New Mexico

—world hunger

—federal budget cuts

—legalization of marijuana

—nuclear warfare

She was surprised. She had thought kids would be interested in a world closer at hand. Then again, maybe that is the world close at hand to those students.

There's a wonderful song from *Monty Python and the Holy Grail* that begins:

Just remember that you're standing
 on a planet that's evolving
And revolving at 1000 miles an hour

It seems to us that this song gets very much to the heart of what we'd like to help young people learn today. For they surely do need to come to grips with the fact that they are passengers on a globe that is changing and evolving at an amazing rate. The trick in doing this kind of teaching is to awaken their interest in the earth as a whole, as a globe, and in their place on it. For us this is global education.

Global educators take on quite a task. Helping students know their world raises some difficult questions:

1. What's worth knowing about the world?

2. Are there basic things about the world that everyone should know?

3. What is possible to know?

The Themes

We build our work around a set of themes which serve as a framework for pursuing such questions. In our opinion, learning about their world should help students to:

—increase their state-of-the-planet awareness

—develop perspective consciousness

—value diversity

—live responsibly with others

—understand world issues and trends

—expand their capacity to change

These themes may not be comprehensive; however, they have been very useful to us in orienting our work. The activities in this book are organized on the basis of these themes, and we're going to briefly elaborate upon each.

Increasing their state-of-the-planet awareness: Students need to understand how the world works, the conditions in which people live, how resources are distributed, and how one interprets information about these subjects. For example, in the decade from 1980 to 1990, global food production increased, yet in the same decade the numbers of people facing starvation also increased. Currently, one of every two humans on the planet lives in Asia. Students need to explore facts such as these and speculate on what they may mean for the future of our species and for the planet.

Developing perspective consciousness: Educated people today need to be aware that their view of the world is only one of many. As one friend puts it, how you see the game depends a lot on your seat in the stadium. Teachers need to help young people become conscious of their own worldview. Once students have clarified their beliefs, they can begin to imagine how others might see things differently; they can try to understand and empathize with people who see things from a different angle.

Valuing diversity: We advocate more than gentle encouragement of tolerance. We want students to be actively and positively engaged in the appreciation of diversity. We want them to see that much of life's fun comes from sharing and enjoying our differences. Moreover, diversity strengthens us. It is interesting to note, for instance, that one principle of ecology is that diversity increases the viability of ecosystems. Systems with very little diversity are more susceptible to external attack, such as from a single predator or a particular virus or a change in climate.

Living responsibly with others: We explore the tension between individual needs and the common good. We hope students will come to appreciate the value of acting in support of the common good because many of the issues that we deal with as global educators are issues of the commons (that which belongs to all of us)—rain forests, pollution, security. To us, building skills for living in the world community is a central task for global educators.

Understanding world issues and trends: All of the facts our students learn and the forces at work in the world on which their studies focus have consequences. Human beings are affected by what is going on in the world, by its diversity, and by what is happening among and between its people. Behaviors and relationships change and evolve in response to these things. Students need to be aware of the trends that the global community is facing—the thinning of the ozone layer, for example, or the widening gap between rich and poor.

Expanding the capacity to change: Change is inherent in any learning experience, of course; so, in a sense, we simply advocate expanding the capacity to learn. But beyond that obvious need is the fact that today's students find themselves in a world that is not only changing but in which the change is unprecedented. Many experts claim that people today have to adapt to changes which come more quickly and in larger numbers than at any previous time in human history.

We have two additional reasons for focusing on the importance of the ability to change and adapt. First, our reading of the state of the planet leads us to think that not only are we in the midst of radical changes brought about by forces more or less beyond our control, but that there are many aspects of life today which themselves demand to be changed. Responsible citizens must know how to meet the challenges such a volatile environment places before them. Second, in a world that is characterized by diversity rather than homogeneity, people must be able to change and adapt just to stay in touch with reality. At the same time, we wish to acknowledge two tensions. There are times when people are asked to change in order to accommodate to the harmful demands of organizations. In cases like this, clearly the burden for change ought to be on the organization, not the individual. Similarly, the demand for individuals to change in the face of diversity may turn out to be a demand for conformity rather than a need for growth. That people are capable of adapting does not necessarily mean that they ought always to adapt.

Global education is in many ways a big and difficult undertaking, and we don't for a moment want to diminish it. We have, however, found some fairly quick and easy ways to enhance the undertaking, to create for young people (or any group of learners for that matter) openings, beginnings for developing their own global perspectives.

International Education and Global Education: The Difference

Our work on this book has brought us a new awareness of the distinction between global education and international education. Probably all good international education is global, but, as the elaboration of our themes above makes clear, not all good global education is necessarily international.

Before students can develop their international understanding, they need to become willing to think globally. They must come to understand the way systems work and interact. They need to build a tolerance for difference and for the paradoxes and ambiguities of life. They must learn to value variety and mystery and to be tolerant of answers that are less than complete and certainly not the only right ones.

We have heard it said that each cultural group thinks its place is at the center of the world; each of us thinks we dwell in the middle kingdom. Global education begins when we encounter the possibility that the middle kingdom is not just where *we* are, but everywhere. Some of the activities in this book are not overtly international, but in our experience all of them can work to help people think more globally, to be open to more of life and the world.

What to Use with Whom

For each activity we have made note of the earliest age at which we think it can be used. Those who work with very young students will find there are fewer activities that seem to apply. One reason for this is that very young students often do not grasp the concept of nations and countries distant from their own. Encouraging young children to be kind and empathetic, to be respectful of nature, to be open and brave in the presence of the new, the unfamiliar, and the different is the beginning of global education. We suspect that many of the activities for older students could be reworked for the younger making use of differences in the child's immediate environment at school, at home, and in the local community, and we encourage you to try.

In our experience, any of the activities that a fourth grader finds enjoyable and stimulating will also capture the interest of adults. For instance, the balloon game, which is one of our most raucous and active offerings, was a great success with a morning Kiwanis group in Iowa. Since all three of us have worked extensively with a wide range of people, we hold to this position even in the face of great skepticism from some. Therefore, we have put no upper limit on the applicability of any activity.

Seymour Fersh, one of the early leaders in the world of global education, claimed that as a teacher he knew he was succeeding when a student raised her hand and said, "This may not be related, but what you just said made me think...." That is what our activities are intended to do, to make people think. We find most people respond when we invite them to think.

And Finally, a Light Touch of Philosophy

If you add up the years we three have spent intentionally involved in global education, it totals more than a half-century. We thought it was time to collect and share a number of the activities that we have developed. So this book contains dozens of activities we have found to be useful and effective in awakening people's interests in learning more about the world and their place in it. We hope you find them helpful and as much fun as we have.

By way of concluding this introduction, we want to share with you something of our approach to teaching and to the work of the educator. The following notions reveal much about our philosophy of education and our epistemology. Over the years, teaching has taught us a number of things. We list them here to give you some sense of the spirit that went into developing the activities in this book and of the way we use them.

Things Teaching Taught Us

Most of us learn early and well that we're inadequate, sinful, unattractive, and not as smart as most other people. If you want to help people become competent, you're going to have to give them lots of opportunities to practice feeling competent.

> Luckily teachers don't have to have all the answers; they don't even have to have most of the answers.

> No one deserves more respect than anyone else.

> It's even possible that everyone could be worthy of an A.

> Teachers can't learn for their students; the students have to do that for themselves.

> You can't make people learn something they don't want to learn, and you can't keep them from learning something if they want to learn it badly enough.

> Learning can take place even when the teacher is somewhere else.

> Learners who are loved are most likely to learn.

The same information means different things to different people. Therefore, conflict is inevitable; thank heavens it can also be productive.

Activities in the classroom are useful for self-discovery and should help students have "ah-ha" experiences; don't use activities to manipulate student thinking.

The exchange of ideas is often a noisy process.

There can be more than one right answer or solution, and there are always lots of options.

Some people are linear thinkers, others aren't; but everybody thinks somehow.

To discuss ideas thoroughly takes as much time as it takes and not necessarily just a class period.

Everybody should have a chance to talk; use big groups, small groups, and times when every single person has a turn if she or he wants it.

Sometimes it's helpful to try to answer your own question.

Most people will work hard on a project if they understand its value, but hardly anyone likes busywork.

Dancing and singing and drawing pictures helps people think better.

Reason and compassion are always compatible.

It's OK to laugh, have fun, and work hard.

In a circle, everyone sits in the front row.

STATE-OF-THE-PLANET AWARENESS

We have two objectives for this section: to review the kinds of knowledge we think students should possess about the world and to offer a number of techniques for helping students acquire it.

We asked in the introduction if there were basic facts everyone should know. We think so. Of course, the content of that basic knowledge is somewhat dependent upon grade level and student interest. What constitutes basic facts for a high school student is substantially different from what it is for a first grader. And all of us need to keep in mind the fact that it is not possible for any single human to know every fact. That is why we need one another.

Nevertheless, by the time students leave high school, they ought to possess knowledge about the amazing variety of conditions in which people live, how resources are distributed, how social structures work, and how one interprets information about these subjects. "The World in the Classroom," "State-of-the-World Test," and "The Human Map" provide a good sense of the sorts of things we think students ought to know.

Of the two objectives mentioned above, our emphasis is on the second. We are particularly interested in suggesting strategies to actively involve students in gaining and interpreting factual knowledge. The "State-of-the-World Test" demonstrates how to combine a conventional exam format with a cooperative learning technique. "The World in Your Grocery Store" and "Global Scavenger Hunt" offer pleasant variations on the field trip. "The World in the Classroom" and "The Human Map" illustrate two different methods for moving students about the classroom to depict how things—such as countries and resources—are distributed in the world.

For the young student, "The Global Apple" is one method by which a teacher can effectively use a concrete object to illustrate some rather abstract notions. "Global Name Puns" is a lighthearted, some might say silly, technique that demonstrates how you can put the students' enjoyment of play to serious purpose. "Planning a Trip" has proven quite successful at the elementary grade level as a means to involving students in studying about other countries, while "Arguing with Maps" has been equally successful at the upper grade levels.

2

The World in the Classroom

What percentage of the world's population lives in Asia? What percentage lives in the United States? What percentage of the world's population speaks Russian? What percentage cannot read, does not have drinking water at home, or suffers malnutrition? These sorts of questions are critically important because the answers give us a basic sense of the state of the world. When presented as statistical tables or any other form of written information, students typically have difficulty remembering the information because it is so abstract, so "out there." If students can actually see how things are distributed over the earth, can actually participate in the distribution through a simulation, they are more likely to remember. And even if they can't recall the actual numbers after a relatively short period of time, having actually "seen" and been part of the distribution they are likely to recall that a lot of things are distributed in very skewed ways.

What we want to do with this activity is to move the students in the class around to illustrate the way the things of the world are distributed. The simplest way to do this is to have all the students stand together at one end of the classroom. Then, based on the data in the chart, move the appropriate number of students away from the cluster. In some cases, population distribution for instance, it is best to move everyone into one or another subgroup at the same time, so Asia is under the clock, North America by the pencil sharpener, etc. After students have experienced population distribution, they reassemble in one part of the room. Then for other items, say "drinking water at home," the students move into a single subgroup to illustrate the point. For instance, let us assume you have 30 students in your class. By using the chart, you have calculated that in your "world," only 9 students have drinking water at home. So you select 9 students and move them away from the full group into a subgroup—after which they reassemble. Now you are ready to select the next subgroup and so on.

Before doing this activity, the teacher can make cards (3 x 5 or 4 x 6) for each item. In the example above you would have a card with the following written on it: "We have drinking water at home." After the 9 students have been moved away from the full group, this card would be given to one of the 9 and read aloud. Sometimes we find this procedure more effective than having the teacher give the data.

We also find it useful to ask the students how they feel about the way something is distributed. They may want to engage in a discussion right then, or you may want to have only a few brief comments made with a fuller discussion or research project to follow later.

4

The World in the Classroom

How Many People	Actual World Percentage	Number in Classroom
1. live in each world region		
Africa	12%	_____
Asia	55%	_____
North America (Canada and U.S.)	5%	_____
Latin America (includes Mexico)	8%	_____
Europe	10%	_____
former USSR	5%	_____
Middle East	4%	_____
Oceania	1%	_____
2. have drinking water at home	30%	_____
3. know how to read	35%	_____
4. have a college education	1%	_____
5. suffer malnutrition	30%	_____
6. are chronically hungry	20%	_____
7. live in urban areas	43%	_____
8. speak English	8%	_____
9. speak Russian	5%	_____
10. speak Chinese (Mandarin and Cantonese)	18%	_____
11. consume 80% of the world's energy	7%	_____
12. own 80% of the farmland	4%	_____
13. are under 15 years of age	33%	_____
14. are over 64 years of age	6%	_____

5

Source: *World Population Data Sheet.* Washington, DC: Population Reference Bureau, 1992.

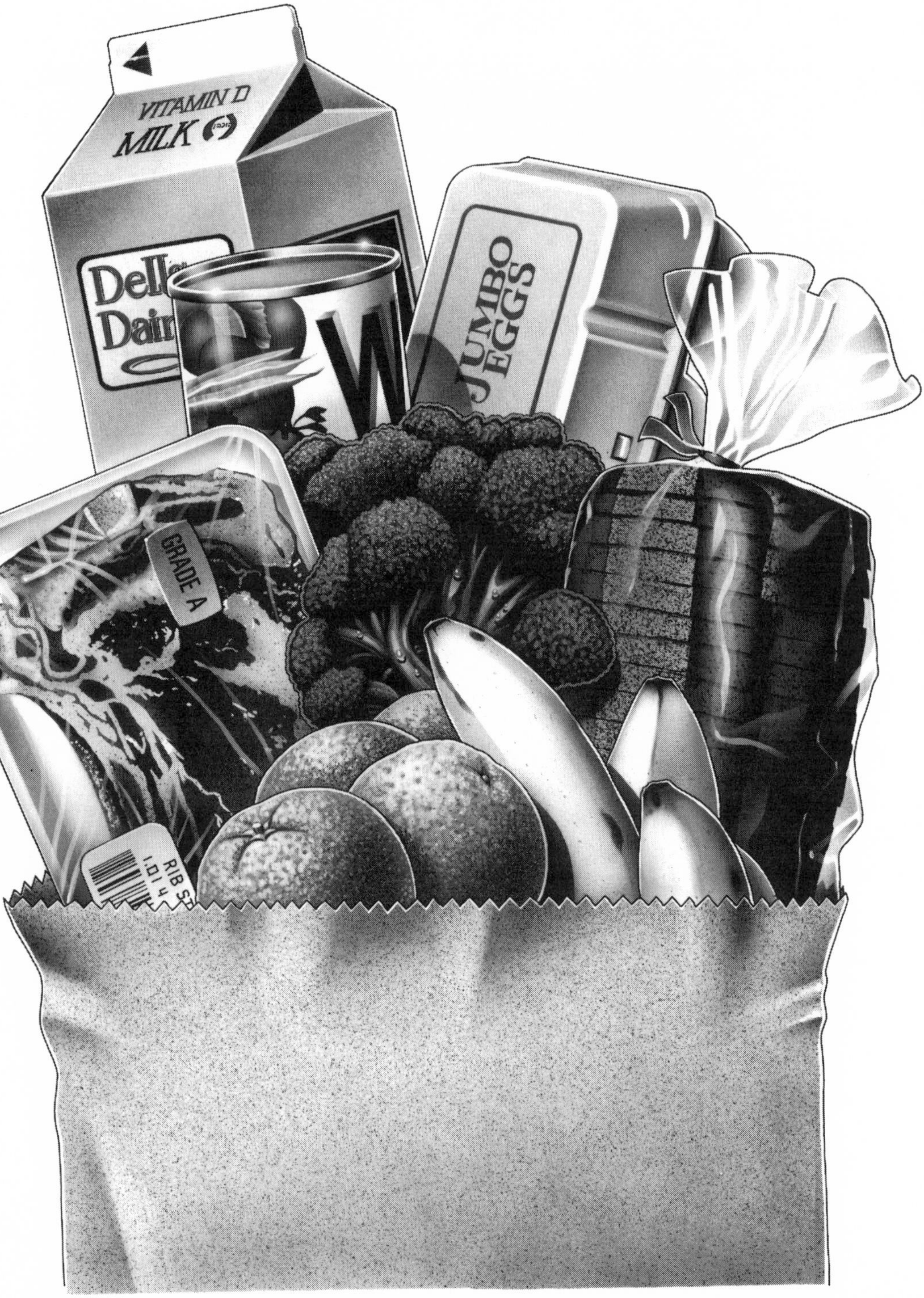
VITAMIN D
MILK
JUMBO EGGS
GRADE A

The World in Your Grocery Store

A trip to the local grocery store or supermarket yields a wealth of global information. And it is a good way to introduce young students to the idea of a world market, without necessarily ever using the term. If the entire class is going to the grocery store together, it is wise to first consult the store manager and ask if she would be willing to help, for instance by telling the students where the various fresh fruits and vegetables come from. Ask if it is okay for students to wander around and read the labels on the packaged goods to see where they were produced.

In the trip to the market, students should be encouraged to collect data about as wide a variety of foods as possible. You could even offer prizes to the person who identifies the most foreign items, the most countries, and the most information that the teacher didn't already know. By interviewing the store manager, and through class discussions and other research, students would learn how and where the food was produced.

As an independent project, some of your students might want to use this exercise as the beginning of a longer research project on the whole food system, from planting to growing to harvesting, to processing, to transporting, to storing, to marketing, to retailing, to consuming. Where do these activities occur? Who does them? Do the people work for themselves or someone else? How much do they get paid? How do they live? It might be especially illuminating to find out how much of the money we spend to buy an item goes to the farmer, to the transporter, and so on.

Variations on this exercise would include trips to a department store, a hardware store, a sporting goods store, and so on. Don't underestimate the power of these trips to bring students more in touch with the world and its impact on their lives.

State-of-the-World Test

We typically think of tests as the way to discover what students learned following a particular unit of study. Sometimes we administer tests before a unit to discover what students know and don't know about the subject. But tests, especially if conducted in a fun way, can be a method for teaching. Here is one test we commonly use at the beginning of workshops for high school students and for teachers. Steve also uses it at the beginning of his introductory Global Politics course. The point of the test is to get students interested in and curious about what is happening in the world.

Here are some suggestions for using the test. Have the students answer the questions in pairs or trios. Items 1, 2, and 3 should be given and answered, in order, before proceeding to the remaining questions.

For Items 1, 2, and 3, tell the students that you will pick a group to give the correct answer. That group gets to continue until it provides an incorrect answer. You will then select another group and proceed in the same fashion. This gamelike format (somewhat like Double Jeopardy), usually makes it more fun for the students.

After item 2 has been completed, remind the participants that approximately 3 out of every 4 human beings live in these 25 nations. It might also be interesting to point out that prior to the recent dissolution of the Soviet Union, 3/4 of the world's population was distributed among only 21 nations.

It is useful, after the test has been completed, to ask students if any of the information surprised them and why. Did some of it bother them? Did it make them angry, sad, happy, or uncomfortable? How might they wish the information differed?

1. Six countries contain 1/2 of the total population of the world. Which are the 6 countries? Write them down in order of population.

   1.   2.

   3.   4.

   5.   6.

2. Another 19 countries account for 25% of the world's people. What are these countries?

1.	2.
3.	4.
5.	6.
7.	8.
9.	10.
11.	12.
13.	14.
15.	16.
17.	18.
19.	

3. The 10 most commonly spoken first languages are:

1.	2.
3.	4.
5.	6.
7.	8.
9.	10.

4. How many languages are there in the world which have at least one million speakers?
    a. 73
    b. 123
    c. 223

5. How many nations were there in 1992?
    a. 288
    b. 188
    c. 88

6. Which nation is home to the largest number of commercial banks?

7. Which nation is home to the most transnational corporations?

8. Between 1970 and 1985, global agricultural (plant and live-stock) production:

    a. declined substantially
    b. declined slightly
    c. remained about the same
    d. increased slightly
    e. increased substantially

9. Between 1970 and 1985, the number of people in the world suffering from malnutrition:

    a. declined
    b. remained about the same
    c. increased

10. Let one dot represent all the firepower used in World War II; this would be the equivalent of 200 Hiroshima-sized A-bombs. How many dots would you need to represent the firepower held in the combined nuclear arsenals of the United States and the former USSR before it dissolved?

    a. 60
    b. 600
    c. 6,000
    d. 60,000

11. Between 1960 and 1987, the world spent approximately $10 trillion on health care. How much did the world spend on the military?

    a. $7 trillion
    b. $10 trillion
    c. $17 trillion
    d. $25 trillion

12. According to the United Nations, what percentage of the world's work (paid and unpaid) is done by women?

    a. 1/3
    b. 1/2
    c. 2/3
    d. 3/4

13. According to the United Nations, what percentage of the world's income is earned by women?

    a. 1/10
    b. 3/10
    c. 5/10
    d. 7/10

14. The nations of Africa, Asia, Latin America and the Middle East, often referred to as the Third World, contain about 78% of the world's population. What percentage of the world's monetary income do they possess?

    a. 10%
    b. 20%
    c. 30%
    d. 40%

12

15. Americans constitute approximately 5% of the world's population. What percentage of the world's resources do Americans consume?

    a. 15%
    b. 25%
    c. 35%
    d. 45%

16. During the twentieth century, average global temperatures have:

    a. risen slightly
    b. basically stayed the same
    c. fallen slightly
    d. fallen significantly

State-of-the-World Test: Answers

1. Six countries contain 1/2 of the total population of the world. Which are the 6 countries? Write them down in order of population: China (1.1b), India (882), the United States (256), Indonesia (185), Brazil (151), Russia (149). (Chinese population is in billions; the others are in millions.)

2. Another 19 countries account for 25% of the world's people. What are these countries? (Numbers in parentheses are in millions.)
   1. Japan (124)
   2. Pakistan (122)
   3. Bangladesh (111)
   4. Nigeria (90)
   5. Mexico (88)
   6. Germany (81)
   7. Vietnam (69)
   8. Philippines (64)
   9. Iran (60)
   10. Turkey (59)
   11. Italy (58)
   12. United Kingdom (58)
   13. France (57)
   14. Thailand (56)
   15. Egypt (56)
   16. Ethiopia (54)
   17. Ukraine (52)
   18. South Korea (44)
   19. Myanmar (Burma) (43)

3. The 10 most commonly spoken first languages are*: (Numbers in parentheses are in millions.)
   1. Mandarin (885)
   2. English (450)
   3. Hindi (367)
   4. Spanish (352)
   5. Russian (294)
   6. Arabic (202)
   7. Bengali (187)
   8. Portuguese (175)
   9. Malay-Indonesian (145)
   10. Japanese (126)

*According to the *World Almanac* (1992).

4. How many languages are there in the world which have at least one million speakers?

    a. 73
    b. 123
    c. 223 (correct)

5. How many nations were there in 1992?

    a. 288
    b. 188 (correct)
    c. 88

6. Which nation is home to the largest number of commercial banks? *Japan*

7. Which nation is home to the most transnational corporations? *United States*

8. Between 1970 and 1985, global agricultural (plant and livestock) production:

    a. declined substantially
    b. declined slightly
    c. remained about the same
    d. increased slightly
    e. increased substantially (Correct: about 35%. Since 1985 changes have become more erratic due to a number of political, economic, and climatic factors.)

9. Between 1970 and 1985, the number of people in the world suffering from malnutrition:

    a. declined
    b. remained about the same
    c. increased (Correct: estimates vary—up anywhere from 5 to 15%, and has continued to increase since 1985.)

10. Let one dot represent all the firepower used in World War II; this would be the equivalent of 200 Hiroshima-sized A-bombs. How many dots would you need to represent the firepower held in the combined nuclear arsenals of the United States and the USSR before it dissolved?

    a. 60
    b. 600
    c. 6,000 (correct)
    d. 60,000

14

11. Between 1960 and 1987, the world spent approximately $10 trillion on health care. How much did the world spend on the military?

    a. $7 trillion
    b. $10 trillion
    c. $17 trillion (correct)
    d. $25 trillion

12. According to the United Nations, what percentage of the world's work (paid and unpaid) is done by women?

    a. 1/3
    b. 1/2
    c. 2/3 (correct)
    d. 3/4

13. According to the United Nations, what percentage of the world's income is earned by women?

    a. 1/10 (correct)
    b. 3/10
    c. 5/10
    d. 7/10

14. The nations of Africa, Asia, Latin America and the Middle East, often referred to as the Third World, contain about 78% of the world's population. What percentage of the world's monetary income do they possess?

    a. 10%
    b. 20% (correct)
    c. 30%
    d. 40%

15. Americans constitute approximately 5% of the world's population. What percentage of the world's resources do Americans consume?

    a. 15%
    b. 25%
    c. 35% (correct)
    d. 45%

16. During the twentieth century, average global temperatures have:

    a. risen slightly (Correct: about .7 degrees Celsius; a growing consensus is that this is the greenhouse effect.)
    b. basically stayed the same
    c. fallen slightly
    d. fallen significantly

16

The Global Apple

Here is another activity to illustrate the way the basic resources of the world are distributed. It is a simple one, the main point of which is to show how relatively small, and therefore precious, are the habitable and cultivable parts of the earth. This can be an excellent introduction to a unit on physical geography or ecology. It is particularly useful for a discussion of population growth and food production because the activity so graphically demonstrates how relatively little land is available for growing food.

Use an apple to represent the earth. Cut a 1/4 slice; this represents the earth's land mass. Cut this quarter slice in half; this represents the amount (1/8) of land actually inhabited by humans. Take this small slice and divide it into 4 pieces. Each piece is 1/32 of the whole. Select one to represent the amount of land used to produce food and clothing for all of the earth's people.

Having each student slice an apple as you give him or her the information will greatly increase the likelihood the student will remember. (Of course, you must determine whether there is any danger in letting your students use knives.)

Once the activity has been completed, invite the students to talk about or write or draw the thoughts and feelings they have in response to this news about the planet.

Global Name Puns

At one of the student leadership conferences we held at Las Palomas, we were playfully helping some young people figure out the 20 most populous nations. While trying to give clues, one of the participants made up a pun using the name of one of the countries: "Pack his tan (Pakistan) suitcase." Then we added, "Philip pines for his lost love." And suddenly a new game was under way. After 10 minutes or so, some of the kids started trying to get multiple puns in a single sentence. The students never ran out of ideas for the next half hour. Here are some of our favorites:

> *Ken ya loan me fifty cents?*
>
> *Pass the Turkey; I'm Hungary.*
>
> *Sur, I name you John.*
>
> *I'm really Mad; a gas car is expensive.*
>
> *I got hit In do nes, ia!*
>
> *E gypt me fifteen cents.*
>
> *I ran to the store.**

It's truly a wonderful, and teachable, moment when kids offer to play a game with you as a way of learning about the world.

There are some 188 nations in the world today. How many can you and your students turn into a pun? Besides countries, many other important global geographic, political, and social categories could be explored, such as world cities over one million in population, the capitals of countries, or rivers or mountain ranges.

---

*But take care that they don't learn wrong pronunciations! Have them note that the actual pronunciation of Iran, for instance, is "ear-ron."

Global Scavenger Hunt

Here is another way to document the links between your community and the rest of the world. We call it a global scavenger hunt and have had a lot of fun using it with junior high and high school students, college students, and adults.

George had a particularly interesting experience using this activity when he was teaching eighth graders and the class was studying perceptions of the Arabs. The students were complaining that there weren't enough materials available about the Arabs, so George designed a scavenger hunt. The teams had 5 days to find as many materials or artifacts relating to Arabs as they could in the community. Five days later the winning team brought back 1,100 items, including a man from Saudi Arabia.

The point of the activity is to send teams out to have them document the connections between the community and the rest of the world or a particular region of the world. You could do this in several ways. One way would be simply to send teams into the community, give them a time limit, and ask them to find as many different examples as they can of the connections the community has to the rest of the world.

Here is another way. Each team can be given a different site—a grocery store (if you wanted a refinement of "The World in Your Grocery Store"), a hardware store, a clothing store, and so on—and told to find as many items as it can that were produced outside the United States or in some assigned country. They can document the source of the items by interviewing the store manager, by writing down information from the packages, clothes, and so forth, or by whatever other (legal) technique they can think of. Teams can be of any size but our experience is that 4, 5, and 6 are optimal. However, remember that when the hunt is completed, students are going to want to talk about and share their experiences. The more teams you have, the longer the sharing will take.

Another alternative is to send teams to different sections of the town. Obtain several maps of the area, divide the maps so that each section includes a number of commercial establishments, and then assign one team to each section.

Still another alternative is to give every team the same list of items to locate. The team which locates and documents the most items (perhaps in some cases by bringing the item back) within some set period of time wins. Below is a partial list of the kinds of items we have had students and educators try to find.

After the hunt is over and you have had the students "show" what they have found, be sure, as mentioned above, to allow them time to talk about the experience and what they learned and how they feel about the hunt. What sorts of problems did they run into? What were their best experiences? What conclusions can they draw from what they found? How would they characterize or what can they say about the connections between the United States and the rest of the world?

Possible Scavenger Hunt Challenges

1. Find a Chinese magazine.

2. Bring back currency from 10 different countries.

3. Bring back brochures from 4 different multinational companies.

4. Bring back evidence from 3 businesses that they trade with 3 other nations.

5. Find a clothing store that sells only Made in America clothes.

6. Find 10 toys or games that originated in another country.

7. Find at least one food item from 50 different countries.

8. Find 2 people who have voted in a national election in another country at some point in their life. Who was running? What were the issues?

9. Find 12 hats from different cultures or nationalities.

10. Find someone who was in Vietnam during the war. What would he or she like you to know about the experience?

11. Find someone who was in Korea during that war. What would he or she like you to know about the experience?

12. Find someone who was in World War II. What would the person like you to know about his or her experience?

13. Bring back a sketch or a description of a sacred symbol for 6 different cultures or religions.

14. Name books currently sold in town by authors from 20 different countries.

15. Name 10 films within the last 5 years that starred a teenager from another country.

16. Find 5 people from other countries. What are 5 things they like about the United States. What are 5 things they don't like?

17. Find 10 places where a written language other than English is displayed.

18. Find 5 different maps of the world drawn before 1900.

19. Bring back evidence that there are groups in town working on major global issues.

20. Find 5 items in town that are made in another country that were not manufactured in that country 5 years ago.

24

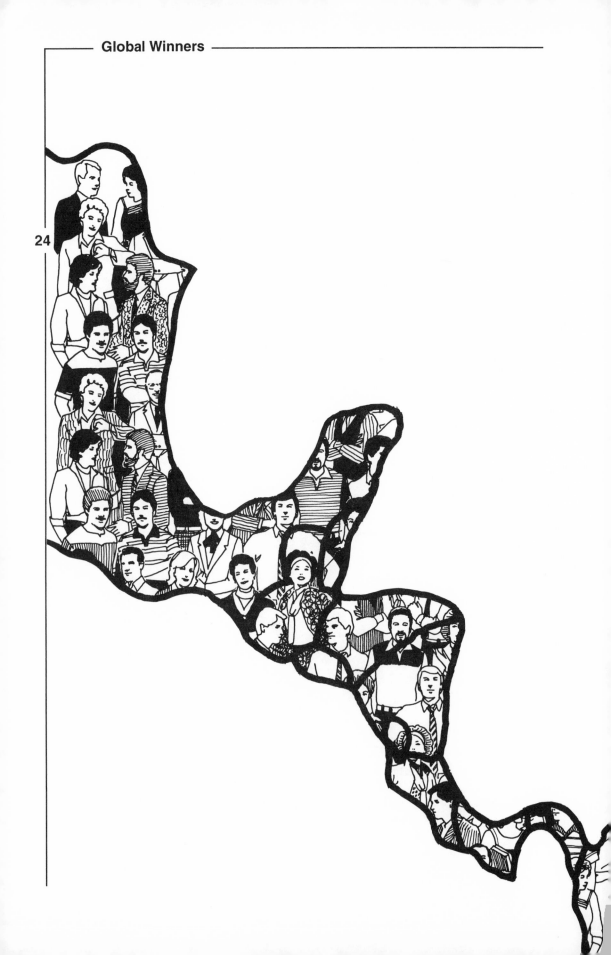

The Human Map

Steve has been teaching about Latin American politics since the early 1970s. At first, he began the course by having the students look at maps. The maps show the various countries, their basic geographical features, and some important historical events. While Steve found the exercise to be useful, he was dissatisfied. It was not quite dramatic enough to make the lesson truly memorable. So he hit upon the idea of a human map. This is an activity that could be adapted for the study of any region or the whole globe.

The activity is amazingly simple, yet effective. Here is how it works. Each student receives a 3 x 5 card with the name of a Latin American country on it. The student with the northernmost country on it is asked to come to the front of the class. (Usually this will be Mexico. However, if the class is large you may need to make it a map of the Western Hemisphere in which the United States or Canada would be northernmost.)

With one student now at the northern point, all the other students are asked to arrange themselves in proper geographic position. Once this is completed, a check is made to see if the arrangement is correct.

But don't stop here. Next, ask a series of questions. The questions are answered by having the appropriate country-person raise his or her hand. By the time you are finished, the students never forget where their country is. Here are some of the Latin American questions:

1. Which country is almost as big as the United States?   *Brazil*

2. Which country was home to the capital of the Incan Empire? *Peru*

3. Which countries are landlocked?   *Bolivia, Paraguay*

4. In which countries is English the offical language?   *Antigua and Barbuda, the Bahamas, Barbados, Belize, Dominica, Grenada, Guyana, Jamaica, Saint Kitts and Nevis, Saint Lucia, Saint Vincent and the Grenadines, Trinidad and Tobago*

5. Which countries are major oil producers?   *Venezuela, Mexico*

6. Which country has gauchos and the pampas?   *Argentina*

7. Which country, if you put it in North America, would stretch from Mexico to Alaska? *Chile*

8. Which country was created as a buffer between Argentina and Brazil? *Uruguay*

9. Which countries contain the Andes mountains? *Colombia, Venezuela, Ecuador, Peru, Bolivia, Chile, Argentina*

10. In which country is Portuguese the principal language? *Brazil*

11. Which country was given to the Dutch by the British in exchange for Manhattan? *Dutch Guiana (Suriname today)*

12. Which two countries share an island? *Haiti and Dominican Republic*

13. Which countries are named for two islands? *Antigua and Barbuda, Saint Kitts and Nevis, Trinidad and Tobago*

14. Which country was home to the Aztec Empire? *Mexico*

15. Which countries are on the Pacific Ocean? *Mexico, Guatemala, Honduras, El Salvador, Nicaragua, Costa Rica, Panama, Colombia, Ecuador, Peru, Chile*

16. Which country had an elected president overthrown by the CIA in 1954? *Guatemala*

17. Which country once had a president from Tennessee? *Nicaragua*

18. Which country is "home" to the potato? *Peru*

19. Which countries have won the World Cup (in soccer)? *Argentina, Brazil, Uruguay*

20. Which countries have been invaded by U.S. troops since 1960? *Cuba, Dominican Republic, Grenada, Panama*

21. Which countries sent troops to the Allies in World War II? *Brazil, Mexico*

22. Which country did John F. Kennedy say the following about: "Geography has made us neighbors, tradition has made us friends"? *Mexico*

23. Which countries are on the equator? *Brazil, Colombia, Ecuador*

24. Which country has the highest population density in the Western Hemisphere? *El Salvador*

25. Which country is the major cocaine producer and supplier? *Colombia*

26. Which country has no military?   *Costa Rica*

27. Which country participated in starting a missile crisis in 1962?   *Cuba*

28. Which country has elected a person of Japanese descent to be president?   *Peru*

29. Which country received the most foreign aid from the United States in 1990?   *El Salvador*

30. Which countries are more urban than the United States?   *Argentina, Chile, Uruguay, Venezuela*

27

   Steve has found that the best way to read the questions is to stand on top of the desk. This activity can be adapted for any sort of lesson involving geographical and historical information.

Planning a Trip

One way to get young students interested in and excited about the world is to have them plan a trip. There are a number of ways you can do this. One way would be for you, through books, pictures, slides, and other resources, to talk briefly about a few different countries in different parts of the world. From these, each student chooses the country he or she would most like to visit. Students should be grouped by their choices. Each group then plans a trip: how do they get their passports, are visas required, what kinds of shots do they need, what forms of transportation would they take, what language would they need to learn, what would they visit once they got there—what are the large cities, important historical sites, interesting natural sites, and so on? Travel agents, consulates, and the local city or college library might all be useful sources of information. You may be able to find people in the community who have lived in these countries; they could be interviewed by the students.

Teachers in schools in Turlock and Hilmar, California, have developed an interesting variation on the travel theme through what they call "carousel days" and "passport days." The idea of the "carousel" is that each class does research on a particular country: its flag, pictures of scenic areas, cities, villages, the people, songs, food, and so on. All these materials are brought into the class, which becomes the country. Then, on certain days, the students travel from country to country enjoying the sights, sounds, and food while learning about some of the customs and a little of the language.

Another idea that is equally fun and challenging is called The Passport. Each student receives a "passport" which contains a space for his or her picture, name, date of birth, and address. The rest of the passport contains a number of questions about a particular country, such as what language do they speak, what is the name of their money, what is the name of the capital city? When these have been correctly answered, the student gets the passport stamped and then, in some version of a carousel day, the student is permitted to travel to the country stamped on the passport. Or the passport can contain questions about several countries, thereby permitting travel to those countries. Students have become so involved in the activity that teachers have had queries from parents asking if their children are really going to be traveling to Nigeria or France.

Arguing with Maps

This activity has several purposes: to introduce students to a variety of resource materials; to help them organize and write clear, declarative statements; to enable them to use maps to present data visually; and to familiarize them with the nations of the world.

The activity is simple. Provide students with atlases, almanacs, and other reference materials which contain information about the world (several are listed in the Resources section). Using the reference materials, ask the students to propose a declarative or a value statement. For instance, from *Women in the World Atlas* students might propose that women are better represented in government in Norway and Sweden than in any other country. The students might develop these statements individually or in small groups.

After the students have written their statements, have them create maps to present the data supporting their argument. This will require some sort of a coding system by using bar graphs in nations, by color coding countries, and/or by using a system of hash marks. *The New State of the World Atlas, Women in the World Atlas,* and *Third World Atlas* (see Resources section) could be used to demonstrate to students different ways of using maps to present data.

DEVELOPING PERSPECTIVE CONSCIOUSNESS

In the introduction we claim that educated people today need to be aware that their view of the world is only one of many. But before attaining that awareness they need to understand what their own worldview actually is. Once students have clarified their beliefs, they can begin to make comparisons and to imagine how others might see things from a different angle and begin to understand and empathize with them. The activities in this section are designed to help learners increase their consciousness of their own perspectives.

Too often education is structured as if learning is something that happens external to or in addition to one's own attitudes, beliefs, and worldviews. We think this orientation misconstrues the essence of learning. As we understand it, learning works from the inside to challenge and shape one's attitudes, beliefs, and worldview. We propose that the teacher build in activities which increase the students' consciousness of their own view of things and which help them understand how that shapes the learning process.

As in all the other sections of this book, our primary focus is on providing teachers with an array of formats to assist learners in developing their skills. The activities in this section include small-group brainstorming and poster making ("Future Wheel," "The Shape of..."); cross-cultural contrasts ("What Does It Mean to Be Educated?," "What Is 'Developed'?," "The African Farmer and Her Husband"); group competitions ("The Balloon Game"); a political values survey; newswriting ("The Whole Story in Action"); interviews ("International Interviews"); and the use of political cartoons from the world's press ("As Others See Us").

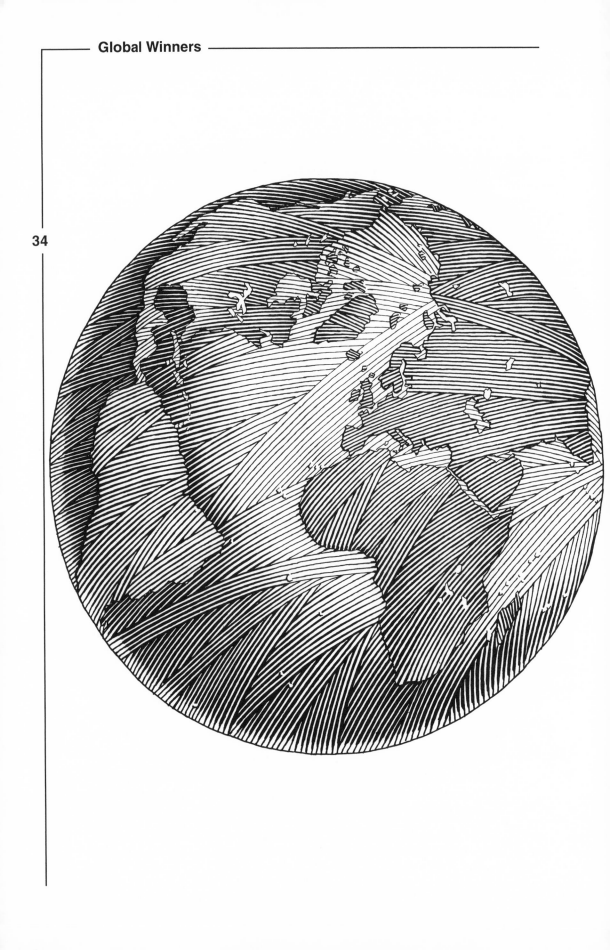

The Shape of...

This is one of our favorite activities. We have used it in primary grades, high schools, colleges, and with senior citizens.

It is especially useful at the beginning of the year or at the beginning of a unit or topic. The primary purpose is to help students get in touch with their worldview—their feelings, biases, and beliefs. The activity communicates to the student and the teacher that learning begins with the students and their current awareness. Since the activity elicits a lot about the students' perspectives, it provides the teacher with a good deal of information about them personally: their fears, their hopes, their misconceptions, their stereotypes. The activity involves both left- and right-brain strengths and a substantial amount of cooperative learning. "The shape of..." can refer to the shape of the world, the shape of Latin America, the shape of the United States, the shape of teenagers—almost anything. We most often use it globally as "The Shape of the Planet." But let us assume you are about to do a unit on Latin America and are going to use this activity to begin the unit. This is how it works:

1. Ask the students to close their eyes and think about Latin America, about conditions in (or the state of) Latin America.

2. As soon as an image pops into their heads, they are to open their eyes and draw the image—or some visual representation of it.

3. After they all have drawn their pictures, randomly assign the students to groups of 5-8 people.

4. In these small groups, students are to explain their pictures to each other.

5. When this step is completed, each group is to draw a group poster incorporating the ideas of each member. Each group should have a large piece of blank paper and several colored markers with which to make the poster.

6. The final step is for each group to tape its poster on a wall and have one or two spokespersons explain the poster to the rest of the class.

No matter what you're examining—your school, a particular country in Latin America, or the planet—the steps are the same, the posters frequently quite beautiful.

This activity has substantial merit in its own right. It can also serve as the basis for longer discussions, an essay, a long-term research project. It's also a wonderful activity for a staff development workshop or the beginning of a teacher's institute.

Ho-Hum, Interesting Fact, That's a Problem

When we read print material, especially charts, graphs, and maps, much of what is remembered is colored by our feelings. In interpreting statistical information, the background and experience of the reader, as well as his or her motivation for acquiring the information, is important in understanding the meaning it has for that person. In this activity, students are encouraged to uncover their own biases toward the information they are reading. It is accomplished by having students categorize information in one of three ways: as ho-hum, an interesting fact, or a problem. Here is one way to go about it.

Give each student several bits of information. This could be a page or two from a statistical report, almanac, or atlas. Several of the other activities in this book contain information sheets which can be used. One of our favorite sources is "Harper's Index," found in each month's issue of *Harper's* magazine. Or you can purchase *The Harper's Index Book.* Another source is the quarterly magazine *In Context,* which now carries a one-page section called "Facts Out of Context" that can also be used. (See Resources section.)

Here are a few examples from some recent issues of "Harper's Index" and "Facts Out of Context":

Thickness of the ozone layer if it were brought down to the earth's surface: *1/4 millimeter*

Estimated number of languages spoken in Africa: *1,000*

Average number of calories burned during an "extremely passionate" one-minute kiss: *26*

Percentage of Africa that is wilderness: *30*

Percentage of North America that is wilderness: *36*

At current rate of population growth, number of years it will take the world's population to double: *41*

Number of nuclear reactors known to be lying on the ocean floor: *50*

Percentage of an Olympic gold medal that is gold: *3*

Rank of IBM among the leading computer export firms in Japan: *1*

Average number of Latin American Catholics who convert to evangelical Christianity each hour: *400*

Estimated annual rain forest clearance worldwide: *80,000 square miles (twice the size of Virginia)*

38

Ratio of rate of Russian deforestation to Brazilian deforestation: *1:1*

Have each student look at his/her sheet(s) of information and classify each item as either "ho-hum" (it is rather boring; who cares?), "an interesting fact," or "that's a problem" (we really ought to do something about this).

If all the students have received the same sheet(s) of information, you could go through each item and ask the students to vote. Tally the votes and note the extent of agreement and disagreement.

If students have received different sheets of information, group the students in twos or threes and have each group read one "ho-hum," one "interesting fact," and one "that's a problem." Students listen to the others explain their categorization, then see if they agree or disagree with the various group choices.

After the voting is completed, or the statements have been read, ask them to clarify their reasoning. Here are some questions you might want to use to guide the discussion:

How much of their response is based on feelings? What kind of feelings?

How much of their response is based on what they think about the world and how it should work?

What accounts for the differences in the responses in the class?

What would have to happen for all the students to respond to the data in the same way?

If all, or a majority, of the students respond to the data in the same way, does that mean their interpretation is the right one?

What other categories can the students suggest for evaluating the data?

A final note—voting isn't necessary. This activity usually sparks good discussion about the information's clarity and accuracy and about the issues raised by the information.

The African Farmer and Her Husband

A father and a son were in a terrible automobile accident. Their injuries were so severe that they were taken to separate hospitals. The son required immediate surgery, so a leading surgeon was rushed in. The surgeon walked into the operating room, looked at the patient, and said, "I can't operate on this boy. He's my son." How could this be true?

The answer, of course, is that the surgeon was the boy's mother. But when we think of surgeons, or doctors in general, we unfortunately do not generally expect them to be women.

For all that has been written about the reforms needed to obtain gender equity, and for all the changes that have occurred, it seems to us that far too many people still think of men as the bosses and the leaders and of women as the secretaries, nurses, and housewives.

Here are two stories that illustrate some rather serious consequences of behaving according to faulty assumptions about gender roles. Read the stories to the students and see if they can fully explain the curious result, the apparent anomaly.

The first comes from Iowa. One of the pesticide manufacturers, in an effort to be sure that its product was used safely, held seminars for Iowa farmers. It taught the farmers how to handle the pesticide, it told them how long to stay out of the area after application, and it told them how to clean up after pesticide use. The company was troubled because even after the seminars there continued to be numerous incidents of pesticide misuse and ensuing complaints. Why? The answer was that women typically weren't invited to the seminars.

On a family farm, quite often the women work in the fields; they also usually oversee the children, do much of the cleanup, and most of the laundry. Unless the man who attended the seminar shared the information fully with his partner, she may not have known that the children should keep away from the area long after the work had been completed, that she should be sufficiently careful with the pesticide herself, and that there was a laundering procedure to properly eliminate pesticide residue.

The second story is also about farming and comes from the African continent. A United Nations development agency provided training in appropriate farm technology to all of the men in one African village. After the training was completed, it was discovered that no change or improvement in farming took place. Why? The title of this activity and the information in the chart on the following page should provide some clues.

This activity almost always elicits strong emotional response. We recommend allowing time for students to discuss what puzzles them. What experiences have they had where their conditioning about gender roles resulted in misunderstanding or mistakes? Be careful not to shout down male students who will have stories of reverse discrimination.

Another way to get students considering the issue of gender and roles is to have them go to magazines and cut out ads using women, ads using men, and ads using both. How are they portrayed? What things are each doing? What is the image that is being projected? What is the physical relationship between the man and the woman in ads where both appear?

40

The Division of Labor in the African Agricultural Economy: % of Total Labor Hours

	Men	Women
Cut down the forest, stake out the fields	95	5
Turn the soil	70	30
Plant the seeds and cuttings	50	50
Hoe and weed	30	70
Harvest	40	60
Transport crops home from the fields	20	80
Store the crops	20	80
Process the food crops	10	90
Market the excess (including transport to market)	40	60
Trim the tree crops	90	10
Carry the water and the fuel	10	90
Care for the domestic animals and clean the stables	50	50
Hunt	90	10
Feed and care for the young, the men, and the aged	5	95

Source: UN Economic Commission for Africa.

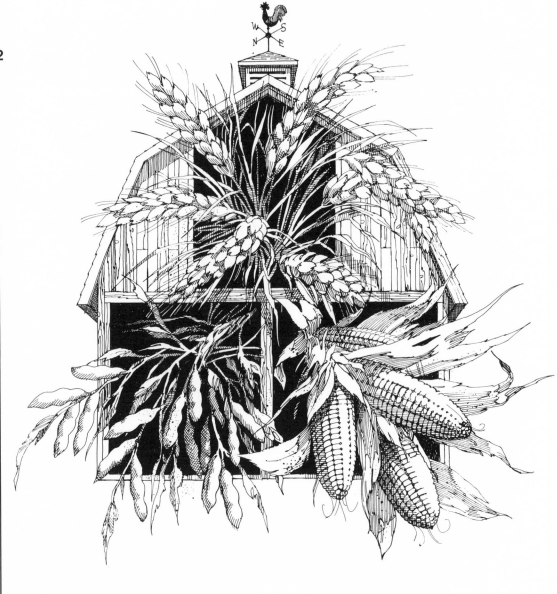

World Food Maze

Puzzles can be an enjoyable way to become familiar with new information or concepts or to review information previously studied. On the next page is a word puzzle which contains the names of 45 vegetables, fruits, and grains. Make copies of the puzzle and hand it to each student or to each pair of students. You can have students do the activity during a class period or as a homework assignment. Note that the instruction on the puzzle says "See if you can find at least 20 of them." You may want to modify this by having them do more or fewer.

After the word search is finished, here are some things you might have the students do. List the foods they have never tried. Have them try one of the foods and look up some basic information about it: where is it grown, what is its nutritional value, to what locale is it native?

Have the students rank-order the foods in terms of nutrition or cost or taste or familiarity, or whatever.

The puzzle could be done in connection with "The World in Your Grocery Store" activity described earlier. Have students do the puzzle word search first, and then see how many of these foods can be found in your local grocery store or supermarket.

The puzzle could also be part of an international food day. After the 45 foods have been identified and after students have learned some information about each, you, or you and several other teachers, could have an international food day. Each student would be responsible for bringing in one of the foods.

Food Maze

The names of 45 vegetables, fruits, and grains are hidden in this maze. See if you can find at least 20 of them.

Circle the foods you find as we did with the word "corn." And write them down on a piece of paper so you can easily keep count. The names may overlap on some letters. You may go vertically, horizontally, or diagonally.

44

```
C  A  U  L  I  F  L  O  W  E  R  I  C  E
P  U  P  E  C  A  N  P  A  P  A  Y  A  G
I  G  C  O  C  O  N  U  T  O  R  E  R  G
N  R  H  U  B  A  R  B  G  P  Y  A  R  P
E  A  S  K  M  T  A  N  P  R  W  S  O  L
A  P  C  A  B  B  A  G  E  U  H  O  T  A
P  E  A  L  I  M  E  L  O  N  E  Y  S  N
P  F  P  E  P  P  E  R  S  E  A  B  P  T
L  R  O  L  R  C  P  N  A  R  T  E  I  O
E  U  T  B  U  B  E  E  T  D  E  A  N  M
N  I  A  T  A  M  F  L  A  T  I  N  A  A
T  T  T  U  R  N  I  P  U  R  O  S  C  T
I  E  O  R  A  N  G  E  O  K  R  A  H  O
L  E  M  O  N  I  O  N  B  A  N  A  N  A
```

Puzzle taken from *UNICEF'S World*, U.S. Committee for UNICEF, 333 E. 38th St., New York, NY 10016. Used by permission.

Future Wheel

Here is a simple exercise for talking about systems and interrelatedness. It comes from an activity developed by futurists Jerry Glenn and Cyndy Guy to help fifth graders explore the consequences of complex problems. As the illustration on the next page indicates, the particular complex problem under discussion was population growth.

The process for creating a Future Wheel goes like this. Students begin by writing down the issue or topic to be discussed or one they would like to discuss. This should be written in the middle of the page. Then, draw a circle around the word(s). The next step is to draw a spoke from the central circle which represents a result or consequence of the initial idea. In the following illustration, the initial idea is "more people in the world," i.e., the world's population will increase in the future. One of the first consequences this person thought of was "more noise." The process of drawing spokes continues until students exhaust the possibilities or until some appropriate amount of time has passed.

While one alternative would be to have the students do the exercise as a homework assignment or as individual work in class, this is clearly an activity that will work best as a group exercise. It's a good chance to demonstrate that all of us together are smarter than any one of us. It can be in a brainstorming format, either in several small groups or with the entire class. Or you might do one large-group brainstorming to give them experience with the process and then have them do another either individually or in small groups.

In the debriefing, start with a general question such as what did they learn or how do they feel about the exercise. Were they surprised by the number of connections they found? Could they prove connections really exist? How?

If you had students do this individually or in small groups, it might be interesting to see if the different Future Wheels could be connected through one or more common spokes.

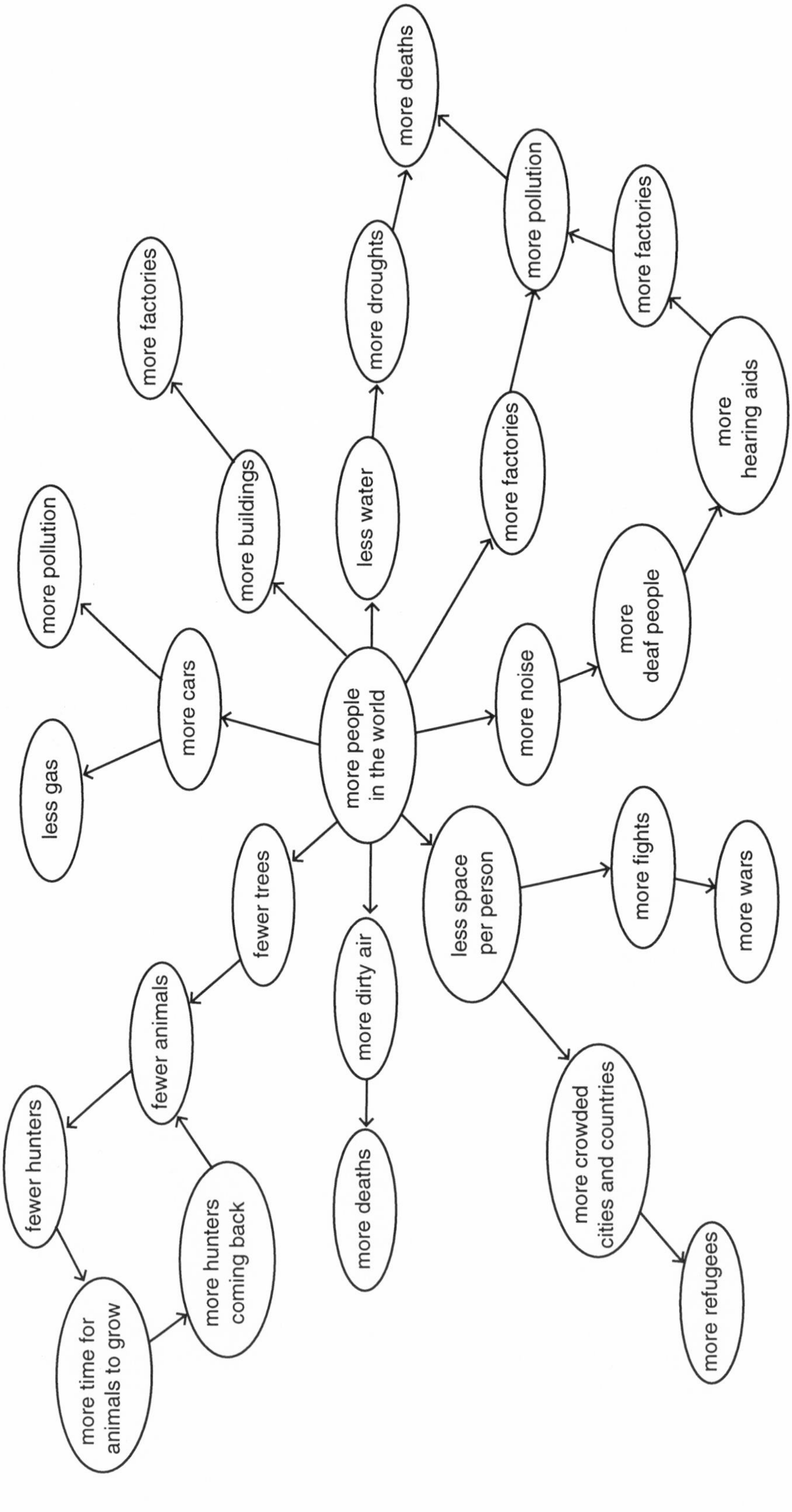
more people in the world
more cars
less gas
more pollution
more buildings
more factories
less water
more droughts
more deaths
more factories
more pollution
more deaths
more noise
more deaf people
more hearing aids
more factories
fewer trees
fewer animals
fewer hunters
more time for animals to grow
more hunters coming back
more dirty air
more deaths
less space per person
more fights
more wars
more crowded cities and countries
more refugees

What Does It Mean to Be Educated?
A Cultural-Historical Perspective

Our friend Joyce Buchholz developed this activity as a way to examine what authorities in various cultures assume constitutes an educated person. As you can see from the activity, though, this is much more than a cross-cultural study of education. By examining educational values we also begin to understand what a culture considers to be important.

Below are listed the critical elements and goals of formal schooling for three different cultures: Renaissance Italy, colonial Massachusetts, and postrevolutionary China. Ask your students to read each of the descriptions and identify the knowledge, skills, and attitudes that were important for students in those cultures to learn. After each has made a list, place the students in groups of three or four to construct a single group list to be reported to the class.

Following the report, there are several questions you can ask which will form the basis of a lively discussion.

- Which knowledge, skills, and attitudes appear most frequently across cultures? Why?

- Are there any which are unique to a particular culture? Why do you think this is so?

- Does it appear that the education being described is designed to teach everyone or only people from certain groups or social classes? Why? Are the interests of any particular individual, group, or institution being served by such an education? Are identifiable interests not being served?

- Which educational systems seem most alike? Which most different?

- What inferences would your students make about what is valued in each culture given what the schools want their students to learn?

- Which culture seems most like ours? Why? Which seems most unlike ours? Why?

Renaissance Italy—15th and 16th centuries

1. The student must be proficient in reading, writing, and ciphering so that he may carry out his commerce successfully. Young men must also understand the law so that they will not be cheated in partnerships, trade agreements, or in the writing of their wills.

2. An educated gentleman will study the grammar, rhetoric, history, and moral philosophy of the ancients in their original languages, for therein lies the font of human wisdom. He shall study Aristotle for physics, Galen for medicine, and the sculpture and arts of Greece and Rome for his aesthetic understanding of the perfection of the human form. He shall study Cicero in particular, for persuasive speech will be especially useful for his work in public affairs.

3. As with the ancients, a man shall be competent in *all* facets of his life so that he may control his own destiny. Physical education is an essential part of the curriculum, for a vigorous body complements a vigorous mind. The gentleman should ride, hunt, and engage in sporting activities. It should be remembered how many illustrious men—Caesar and Alexander among them—have been good swimmers. The game of chess, while not physical, improves one's understanding of tactics for use in commerce and on the battlefield.

4. Students shall learn the art of conversation, good manners, and personal charm so that they may deal effectively in polite society.

5. The student will learn that it is also his duty to serve his community, for only then, in good conscience, may he pursue with vigor the profits of commerce which will assure his prosperity.

6. Students should learn to deal ethically and justly with others in their dealings, at least to the extent that it is practical to do so.

From *Renaissance.* John Hale. New York: Time, Inc., 1965.

Massachusetts Bay Colony, 17th century

1. The student shall learn to read from the *New England Primer* so that he may begin to know the truths of the Scriptures. When he has mastered reading and writing, he shall continue to learn the laws set down for us by God in his Holy Writ, working out his salvation under the purity and power of Biblical ordinance.

48

2. The student will give his full allegiance to the laws of God, the laws of England, and the British crown. He shall understand that those who do not follow these laws are agents of Satan who will be banished from our community.

3. Students shall participate fully in the planting and harvesting of crops and in all our efforts to build and defend the community. They shall participate from childhood in daily worship and look upon their fellows with good will and brotherly affection.

4. Students shall be taught that simplicity of life requires simplicity of dress and that pride, extravagance, idleness, immoral behavior, desire for wealth, alcohol, sleeping at sermons and breaking the Sabbath are the work of the Devil.

5. The student will come to learn that we have built our City upon a Hill that we may be as a beacon to all those who would live in covenant with our Lord.

From *The National Temper: Readings in American History.* L. Levine and R. Middledauff, eds. New York: Harcourt, Brace, 1968.

The People's Republic of China, 1950s and 1960s

1. Students shall have a *useful* education, learning the methods of modern agriculture, industry, science and technology so that our country may prosper and progress. Too long have students been required to study the esoteric "wisdom" of the ancients and the classical philosophy of a decadent class society.

2. Students will subjugate their individual interests to the greater good of the people. Too long have the masses been victims of scholar/officials, greedy landlords and Western imperialists. Today's students will lead the way to a classless society.

3. Students will learn that they are not superior to peasants but, instead, that they have much to learn from the dignity of peasant life. Therefore, they will work shoulder-to-shoulder with peasants on the land. All people in our society must be productive. One can't grow rice on a blackboard.

4. Both male and female students will be educated equally for the labor of women is needed if we are to have full productivity. We shall, therefore, be done with child marriage and concubinage. Students shall learn that responsible citizens marry late and limit their families.

49

5. Students shall learn the virtues of austerity, humility, and self-discipline. It is desirable that the human spirit triumph over the decadence of material considerations. Only by eliminating poverty and sharing the wealth of the land with *all* our countrymen will justice and morality prevail.

6. It shall be the duty of the student to learn the rudiments of health care, family planning, nutrition and sanitation so that he/she may improve the lot of the peasantry while imparting basic literacy to all our people.

7. Students shall learn to reject the ideas of the ancients and the ways of their grandfathers and shall seek out reactionary elements within the family and the community for purposes of re-education to the new society.

8. All students shall learn to speak Mandarin so that China may have a common language which will unite the country.

9. Students shall recognize that they are on the frontier of a new society, one that will serve as an example for other Third-World peoples. They shall therefore learn about other cultures to the extent that they have been exploited by the Western imperialists.

From *China: Yesterday and Today.* M. Coye and J. Livingston, eds. New York: Bantam, 1979.

50

The Balloon Game

It seems there is a pervasive human tendency to think that there are only two ways to respond to conflict: fight or leave. We created this activity to help people discover how conditioned we are to compete and to assume that every game has to have winners and losers. Here is how the game works.

Announce that the object of the game is to hang as many balloons as possible on your team's home base. You might even put this in writing and post it where everyone can see. Then divide the group into teams. The minimum number is two three-person teams. Each team must have at least one "hanger," one "emissary," and one "inflater." The game has been played with as many as five teams of eight members. It is important that all teams have the same number of players.

After the teams have been selected, remind the players that the object of the game is to hang as many balloons as possible on the home base of your team. At this point, each team should have a designated home base (something on which a balloon with string can be hung). Next tell everyone the rules of the game. They are pretty simple.

1. Play begins when the game director signals the start and ends with a similar signal from the director.

2. Only *inflaters* may inflate balloons.

3. Only *hangers* may hang the balloons.

4. Only *emissaries* may visit other teams.

5. Emissaries may do only what their team instructs them to do.

Each team receives an equal number of balloons, pieces of string, and as many pushpins as there are emissaries. Before beginning, ask if there are any questions. When answering, refer only to the rules of the game. Do not add information or interpret the rules or goals. After all questions have been answered, tell them the game is now about to begin. Hold your arm up, wait a moment (or glance at your watch as if the game were going to be timed), then drop your arm and say "Begin!"

So far, every group we've ever done this with has very quickly started to inflate its balloons and almost as quickly has sent emissaries to start popping the balloons of the other teams. Allow the chaos to develop for five or ten minutes or until either all the balloons are gone or the level of violence has become threatening. Then stop the game.

Once the action has been stopped, have the students sit in a circle on the floor and discuss what happened. Here are some questions you might ask.

52

1. How do you feel?

2. Did anyone win?

3. What was the object of the game? If many say it was to win or to hang the most balloons, read back to them your original announcement which says the "object is to hang *as many balloons as possible....*"

4. Why did people choose to pop balloons? Or, why didn't they?

5. How might things have gone differently?

6. How could you change the game to make it less competitive?

7. Is the game like life? (Note: Most students will point out that you set them up by giving them pins. That is when this question is appropriate.)

Once you've sensitized your students to our win/lose conditioning, you can begin to explore with them some of the new options and ways of thinking that are available to us today. We very often use games from the books *The New Games Book* and *More New Games!* (see Fluegelman in Resources section) in conjunction with the balloon game. They are also the kinds of activities that are more effective if discussed, and they offer the possibility of fun from cooperating as well as competing.

Global Designs

Worldviews are images, templates, and patterns of believing and thinking that we apply to the world around us. Our images of the planet and its condition help us decide what it means to live responsibly. For example, if we see the world as a machine, we're likely to treat it in one way; if we see it as an organism, we'll treat it quite differently.

We share our assumptions about the nature of the world in many ways. Visual images can communicate our worldview beautifully. For example, "Spaceship Earth," "the brotherhood of humankind," "wholeness," "interdependence," "multiple perspectives," "global society," and other phrases and concepts can be communicated visually.

Here are sample symbols from high school student clubs in two communities where we have worked. The students designed the symbols themselves.

On page 56 are examples we have collected of symbols and logos of organizations that sponsor international projects and support global education. Their symbols are clear attempts to state visually some of the assumptions and ideas that govern the goals and operations of the organization. Here are some questions you can ask the students:

> Can you match the logo with the name of the organization?

> What is your interpretation of the meaning of the design?

> What does it say to you about the group's worldview?

Have the students call or write these organizations to check out their perceptions. They can also collect more examples from other organizations' advertisements in magazines. What are the images and worldviews being portrayed in them? What is the message they are communicating? Why?

Finally, why not have students design some of their own logos that would communicate to others the students' assumptions about how we can or should live together on this planet.

Organizations

1. International Child Resource Institute
   2955 Claremont Ave.
   Berkeley, CA 94705

2. The Center for Human Interdependence
   114 Reeves Hall
   Chapman College
   Orange, CA 92666

3. The Whole Earth Papers
   Global Education Associates
   475 Riverside Drive, Suite 1848
   New York, NY 10115

4. National College of Education
   Center for International Cooperation
   2840 Sheridan Rd.
   Evanston, IL 60201

5. InterAction American Council for Voluntary Intl. Action
   2101 L St. N.W., Suite 916
   Washington, DC 20037

6. Global Tomorrow Coalition
   1325 G St., N.W.
   Washington, DC 20005

7. Global Education: Minnesota (GEM)
   Minnesota International Center
   306 Wesbrook Hall
   77 Pleasant St. S.E.
   Minneapolis, MN 55455

8. Heifer Project International
   PO Box 808
   Little Rock, AR 72203

9. ISAR (formerly Institute for Soviet-American Relations)
   1608 New Hampshire Ave., N.W.
   Washington, DC 20009

10. The Asia Society, Inc.
    1785 Massachusetts Ave., N.W.
    Washington, DC 20036

11. The Heritage Foundation
    214 Massachusetts Ave., N.E.
    Washington, DC 20002

12. American Security Council
    Washington Communications Center
    Reston, VA 22713

13. The Stanley Foundation
    216 Sycamore, Suite 500
    Muscatine, IA 52761

14. Las Palomas de Taos
    PO Box 3400
    Taos, NM 87571

15. United Nations University for Peace
    PO Box 199
    Escazu, Costa Rica

16. Iowa Division, United Nations
    Association of the U.S.A.
    26 E. Market St.
    Iowa City, IA 52240

A.

B.

C.

D.

E.

F.

G.

UNA-USA

H.

I.

J.

K.

SAN SACRAMENTO STREET · FRANCISCO · · CALIFORNIA 94109 · · PROGRESSIVE SPACE FORUM

L.

international child resource institute

M.

AMERICAN SECURITY COUNCIL

N.

O.

P.

Q.

Key: 1. L, 2. J, 3. N, 4. I, 5. H, 6. O, 7. F, 8. Q, 9. K, 10. A, 11. C, 12. B, 13. M, 14. E, 15. P, 16. D, 17. G.

The Whole Story

The purpose of this activity is to explore a common myth—the myth that newspapers and magazines tell the whole story. Many of us have had the experience of being interviewed by a local newspaper only to discover that what we said and what actually was printed were two rather different things. Having our ideas misrepresented may not be a serious problem most of the time, but what if a misrepresentation affects freedom or our livelihoods or national security?

Steve experienced a variation of this. He was in Chile during the presidential election campaign of 1970. This was the election in which the Socialist Salvador Allende won the presidency. During the campaign, Steve frequently would read accounts in *Newsweek* concerning the anti-U.S. violence which was occurring in Santiago—the capital of Chile. In fact, the U.S. magazines generally painted a picture of chaos. Yet, walking around the capital at all times of the day and night, he never encountered any anti-U.S. violence, saw only a couple of pieces of graffiti which even hinted at any negative attitudes toward the United States, and saw only routine campaign rallies and marches. There was nothing resembling chaos. Of course, on occasion a rally would get a little wild and sometimes the police would disband it, but hardly mass chaos and certainly no danger to Americans.

What is particularly interesting about these experiences is that, when we are directly involved in an event and see it reported, we almost always have a host of questions about the story: Why did they emphasize this point and not the other? Why did they use this quote and not another? What significant information was omitted?

On the other hand, when reading an article in the same paper or magazine about which we have no knowledge or in which we were not directly involved, we tend to read it differently. We are inclined to accept that report or story as the truth, the "whole" story.

Susan Sontag, author and film director, says, "Every medium creates a primary illusion." A newspaper's or magazine's primary illusion is that they present the whole, unbiased story. Students who are conscious of this fact are likely to be more critical in their reading. Here are some things you can do to help sharpen this kind of critical thinking in them.

Have students bring in a current newspaper story and then list ten questions they have about the event that the story doesn't answer. Choose a local news story for this exercise and have everybody in the class collect additional relevant information that is not in the newspaper. Have them make sure that the information they gather is verifiable in some fashion and not rumor. For example, students could telephone the parties involved to get their versions.

Have your students do some background research and find alternative views on an international story or a report of something happening in a foreign country.

Have students attend an event that is likely to be the subject of a news report, one that is in the news in advance of the event or one that is regularly covered. Have them compare their perceptions of the event with the newspaper coverage. On what did the paper focus? What did it leave out? Why?

The Whole Story in Action

Here's a follow-up to the previous exercise in which we discussed the notion that a primary illusion of newspapers and magazines is that they provide us with the whole, unbiased story. This is a simulation Steve often uses which requires some of the students to report about an event in which the others have participated.

The setting for the simulation is a school board hearing called to discuss the school budget. Five students play the role of the school board members and listen to brief speeches by other students who play the roles of principal, science teacher, football coach, counselor, fine arts teacher, head of the teacher's union, and so on. The purpose of the speeches is to try to influence the school board in its budget-making process. Two groups of students, three in each group, are also selected to be reporters for two local newspapers. They take notes during the simulation and then each group writes a one-page story.

On the following day, the two stories are read to the class. Both groups typically do a good job and it is important to recognize their effort. (This needs to be emphasized so that the students doing the reporting will not feel they are being personally attacked for having perceptions different from other students.) But the other students will be able to point out numerous pieces of information that were omitted, and most of them will have a different perspective on the tone and feeling of the meeting. Students can see that even under rather good conditions, the very nature of reporting usually prevents anyone from writing the whole story.

An alternative to this would be to play the simulation without assigning the reporter roles. After the simulation is completed, announce that everyone has just been hired by the local "Times" to write a one-page news story about the simulated school board hearing. Students could share their reports or you could read some to the class to illustrate the impossibility of reporting the whole story.

You may prefer to create a simulation that relates more directly to your community or area of study. Assign one or two groups of students to be reporters during the simulation. They should take notes about what is happening. After the simulation, have them write a brief article as if they were writing for a newspaper or magazine. Or have them prepare a TV or radio news broadcast. Have them read the article to the class and then discuss it. Did it omit anything? Do other students have a different feeling about what happened?

Another point to be made is that if the students, who are from the same culture, speak the same language, and share a common set of values, see the event so differently, it is inevitable that students from other cultures and other countries would have even greater divergence in their perceptions of this or almost any incident. In fact, if you have international students we strongly recommend that one or more of them be reporters. Students of different American ethnic groups may also have special perspectives that underline this point.

Good News/Bad News

Here is another format to help students understand how they judge what they read. The activity allows them to explore how initial judgments determine the meaning of data. An equally important objective is to help students see that what is good news to one person can be bad news to another person.

Here are various statements by different "experts" about the state of the world:

- Three governments in five spend more to guard their citizens against military attack than against all the enemies of good health.

- As a contributor to the buildup of atmospheric carbon dioxide (CO_2), the average U.S. resident is worth 16 times a Third-World person, 2.5 times a Japanese, and 3 times a West European.

- It appears that we are moving toward a world economy characterized by regional trading blocs; the principal blocs will be the European Community, the North American Free Trade Area, and the East Asian Trading Area.

- Throughout most of the world, life expectancy is increasing.

- Since 1957, more than 2,000 satellites have been launched into orbit around the earth. About 3/4 of them were put up there for military purposes.

- The United Nations estimates that 60% of the world population will live in cities at the end of the twentieth century.

- The Soviet Union has ceased to exist.

Here are some things you can do with the statements. Have the students read the statements and then discuss or write about the following questions:

- Is the statement good news or bad news?

- From the way the statement is written, do you think the author feels the statement is good or bad news?

- If the statement is good news, what would make it bad? If bad, then what would make it good?

- Who in the international system would consider the statement to be bad news? Why?

- Who would consider it to be good news? Why?

Here is a variation of the activity. Give students copies of a newspaper and red and green markers. Have them use the green marker to circle "Good News" statements in the paper and red to circle "Bad News" statements.

Then ask them to write a supporting paragraph for their evaluation of two or three of the statements. Have the students share some of their responses, either in small groups or before the class. Afterward, discuss some of the following questions:

- Do they think other students would agree with their evaluation? Why?

- Would any additional information change their view?

- Are there certain kinds of words that writers use to try to influence our feelings about information?

- How could the statement be rewritten if the writer wished to convince the reader that it was good news or that it was bad news?

As an alternative to the last discussion question, or as a follow-up, place the students in groups of two or three, give each group one or two statements, and have them rewrite each to:

1. convey the impression that the information is good news

2. convey the impression that the information is bad news.

What Is "Developed"?

The term "development" has become increasingly popular in referring to the process of change in Africa, Asia, Latin America, and the Middle East. And, like many other general terms, it is loaded. What does it mean to be "developed"? To be "underdeveloped"? What is meant by the process of development?

Countries like the United States, Canada, France, and Japan are often referred to as the developed nations. Most of the countries of Asia, Africa, Latin America, and the Middle East are frequently referred to as underdeveloped, developing, or less developed countries (LDCs). Given such a categorization, it seems clear that many people are using "development" in an economic sense. By conventional economic measures, the so-called developed countries are more industrial and wealthier in that their gross national product (GNP) and gross national product per capita (GNP/capita) are larger.

Is this all there is to it? Should countries be satisfied with just economic growth, with more wealth and more economic power? Maybe, because it is possible that overall economic improvement must precede other developments. But it is also possible that economic growth, by itself, isn't enough. And it is even possible that economic growth is the wrong goal. For example, for some people, development refers to projects to help the poor. These projects might include economic redistribution rather than, or in addition to, economic growth. For others, development may mean adaptations which involve minimal disruption of traditional values. A recent UN-commissioned report advocates "sustainable development," that is, economic growth that, in the long run, doesn't damage the ecological and social systems it serves. And there are many other views.

Below are some definitions and statements about the subject by various experts in the area of international development. After giving the students a brief introduction to the concept of development (a short bibliography is provided at the end of this activity), have the students read the following brief statements.

Views of Development

Development is improvement of the quality of life of people; it is not synonymous with economic growth, though such growth is necessary to achieve it. The people whose quality of life needs to be improved are mainly the poor.

—Martin McLaughlin, Interfaith Action for
Economic Justice

The basic goal of development is the attainment of high mass consumption.

—W. W. Rostow, Professor of Economics

Development is a process. No one person, community or nation is fully developed. We are all at different stages of development. Development should always be based on the values of human dignity and justice.

—Nicole Mendoza, Catholic Relief Services

What does development mean? I believe it to be the building of a more equitable society; one in which people have access to the resources to work and prosper.

—Laurence Simon, American Jewish World Service

The question is whether Americans can create policies and institutions that suit an interdependent world—whether they will recognize that the development of countries overseas is a crucial component of their own welfare.

—John Hamilton, World Bank

Agriculture is the key to economic development. Concentration on the family farm is the key to success both in increasing productivity everywhere in the world and in creating a sociopolitical base for a society in which self-reliance, enterprise, and commitment to cohesive family relationships are important.

—Orville Freeman, former U.S. Secretary of
Agriculture (paraphrased)

64

Development is people working together for the well-being of the global community.

—Mary Hill Rojas, Virginia Polytechnic Institute

The environment is a critical variable in the development process. In fact, protection of the life support system, or the ecosystem in which development is taking place, has become one of the most critical factors in the process.

—Helen Vukasin, Development Institute, UCLA

65

I hold that economic progress is antagonistic to real progress....I have heard many of our countrymen say that we will gain American wealth but avoid its methods. I venture to suggest that such an attempt if it were made is foredoomed to failure. We cannot be wise, temperate and furious in a moment.

—Mahatma Gandhi

Follow up with a discussion that considers such questions as: What are the differences between the points of view as expressed by the various authors? With which do you agree? With which do you disagree? Does it make any difference? In what ways is the United States developed or underdeveloped? Alternatively, students might come to the conclusion that the language used in the debate over development is not useful. Is it used, at least in this country, to mean "like the United States," with the assumption that to be more like the United States is to be better, or developed? What we may need to understand is that there are many different ways that a nation or a culture can be "developed."

A different technique for beginning a discussion about development would be to show students pictures of places or scenes from different countries. A good way to provoke controversy is to show pictures which "trick" the student by challenging stereotypical views. For instance, scenes from so-called developed countries might include a bullfight arena in Houston or a sharecropper in Alabama or a mother and children huddled in a doorway in San Francisco. Conversely, you might include pictures of gleaming skyscrapers in Brazil or a nuclear power plant in Argentina or a combine moving down a wheatfield in India.

Some Sources for Talking about Development

Most of the statements under "Views of Development" are taken from "What Does Development Mean," in *The Development Kit,* 1988, Catholic Relief Services, 1011 First Avenue, New York, NY

10022. The Rostow statement is a paraphrase from *The Stages of Economic Growth.* The Freeman quote is from *The Global Economy,* World Future Society, 1985. The Gandhi quote is from *Daedalus,* (Winter 1989).

Daedalus. "A World to Make: Development in Perspective." (Winter 1989).

Joy, Carol, and Willard Kniep. *The International Development Crisis and American Education.* New York: Global Perspectives in Education, 1987.

Goodland, Robert, Herman Daly, and Salah El Serafy. *Environmentally Sustainable Economic Development: Building on Brundtland.* Washington, DC: World Bank, 1991.

Gurtov, Mel. *Global Politics in the Human Interest.* Boulder, CO: Lynne Rienner Publishers, 1988.

In Context. "Dancing toward the Future: 'Environment' and 'Development.' " (Summer 1992).

King, Alexander, and Bertrand Schneider. *The First Global Revolution: A Report by the Council of the Club of Rome.* New York: Pantheon, 1991.

Korten, David. *Getting to the 21st Century: Voluntary Action and the Global Agenda.* Hartford, CT: Kumarian Press, 1991.

MacNeil, Jim, et al. *Beyond Interdependence: The Meshing of the World's Economy and the Earth's Ecology.* New York: Oxford University Press, 1991.

Rostow, W. W. *The Stages of Economic Growth: A Non-Communist Manifesto.* New York: Cambridge University Press, 1960.

Seligson, Mitchell. *The Gap between the Rich and the Poor: Contending Perspectives on the Political Economy of Development.* Boulder: Westview Press, 1984.

Sen, Gita, and Caren Grown. *Development, Crises, and Alternative Visions: Third World Women's Perspectives.* New York: Monthly Review Press, 1987.

Wilber, Charles, ed. *The Political Economy of Development and Under-Development.* New York: Random House, 1988.

66

Similarities and Differences

When some people compare objects, say a pencil and a pen or a car and an elephant, they typically see differences. Others typically will see similarities, and a few will see both similarities and differences. What might account for people using one of these perceptual modes consistently? What learning or experience determines our way of comparing? What motivates people to see only one or the other, and how might they be motivated to see both? Is seeing both similarities and differences the best way to approach the world? If it is (and we think it is), can people learn to see both as a natural way of reacting?

Here's how you might engage your students in exploring these questions. Select some pairs of items to be compared. Start with objects that fall within the animal, vegetable, mineral categories. Don't start with ideas or concepts.

Whether you have each individual write his or her responses or have a few students respond in front of the class or have everyone involved in small groups or pairs, the question that everyone should answer is, "How do these two items compare?" It is important that you not mention the words "similarities" and "differences" in giving the instructions.

Have the students' responses recorded. Then repeat the experiment with another pair of objects. After you've done this three or four times, divide the responses into two categories: similarities and differences.

Then ask each student to consider the ways each individual made comparisons. Did each see mainly similarities between items or mainly differences? Did he or she perhaps see nearly as many differences as similarities?

To help the students understand the particular pattern of perception that they demonstrated in the experiment, have them answer the following question: "What are my reasons for perceiving things the way I did?" If your class is highly motivated, you could have them take quiet (almost meditative) time and think of as many answers to the question as they can. You'll most likely be able to tell by watching them when they have thought of answers. It's probably best to have them write down their answers. After a few minutes, let them share any responses they want with the group. The thrust of this approach is to avoid the quick answer and encourage students to think in depth about how they make comparisons.

Follow this activity with a discussion of the following question: "What are the advantages to seeing both similarities and differences?" In the world today there are many instances where comparisons occur. For example, Japan is compared to the United States, and the Third World is compared to the First World. Do these comparisons focus on similarities, differences, or both? What purpose is served by the different ways of focusing on comparisons?

Sometimes we are asked to compare things that are not appropriate to compare, like apples and oranges. For instance, we are often asked to compare socialism (a particular form of economy) with democracy (a particular form of decision making). Comparisons such as this are typically made for political (ideological) purposes. Are there other sorts of commonly articulated comparisons which are misleading or unfair?

Finally, have your class practice seeing both similarities and differences with some new pairs of objects. Urge them to seek the kinds of comparisons that are most difficult for them. Or they can find partners who see things differently so that they experience how differences in perspective can be enriching.

Political Values Survey

Helping students become aware of their own perspective is a central feature of good global education. There are many ways to do this, and there are lots of activities in this book to help you. Here is one way.

This is a political values survey. The intent of the survey is to provide students with an opportunity to begin thinking about their political values. Surveys such as this are always somewhat frustrating because one is asked to respond to statements with a very limited number of choices. It can also be frustrating because not all important issues are covered by the various statements. In spite of these limitations, we have found that the survey is an excellent way to begin a discussion about the students' political values.

Reproduce the following survey, give one to each student, and ask each to circle the choice that is the closest to what he or she believes. Acknowledge that the statements may be too limited and that, at times, the students may be a little frustrated with the choices. Tell them that this is merely a beginning point for a discussion about political values.

Political Values Survey

For the statements below, circle a 5 if you agree strongly, a 4 if you agree, a 3 if undecided or if you think there is an equal balance between the statement and its alternative, a 2 if you disagree and a 1 if you disagree strongly.

1. By nature, human beings are competitive and rather selfish.

         5   4   3   2   1

2. The right to own property and the right to privacy are more important than the right to economic security and the right to medical care.

         5   4   3   2   1

3. If a socialist government comes to power in another country, even by free elections, and threatens American property interests, the U.S. government ought to overthrow the socialist government.

         5   4   3   2   1

4. A time for voluntary, silent prayer should be a part of the public school curriculum.

         5   4   3   2   1

5. Welfare expenditures must be reduced.

         5   4   3   2   1

6. People on welfare should be required to work.

         5   4   3   2   1

7. Strong economic sanctions against South Africa are unfair and counterproductive.

         5   4   3   2   1

8. Affirmative action is bad policy.

         5   4   3   2   1

9. The Los Angeles riots of 1992 were mostly caused by the loss of family values.

         5   4   3   2   1

10. Federal environmental laws are too harsh, restricting needed economic growth.

5   4   3   2   1

11. We cannot afford deep cuts in military spending because America must remain strong.

5   4   3   2   1

12. Too much money is being spent on public education.

5   4   3   2   1

13. A lower capital gains tax rate would be good economic policy and everyone would gain.

5   4   3   2   1

14. Federal and state governments should not interfere with the sale of handguns.

5   4   3   2   1

15. An equal rights amendment would be unwise.

5   4   3   2   1

Add your numbers and write your total score_____

As you have probably noticed, the statements have been written in such a way that a "strongly agree" response would be on the political right while a "strongly disagree" response would be on the political left. Therefore, the higher the score the more the individual leans to the right; the lower the score the more she or he leans to the left.

> **Note:** In labeling the two ends of the spectrum, we used "right" rather than "conservative" and "left" rather than "liberal" because it could well be argued that someone with a very high score, say in the 70s, has moved to the right of conservative (reactionary; radical right, etc.) while someone with a score approaching zero has moved beyond liberalism to socialism or radical left. In a series called *Opposing Viewpoints* (see Resources section) there is a volume entitled *The Political Spectrum* which is an excellent source of ideas on this subject.

Here are some things you might do once the students have completed the survey. Begin by going over each item. We find it useful to highlight certain of them as being particularly fundamental. What we believe about human nature is one of our most fundamental beliefs. Thus, how people respond to item 1 typically will color almost all their other responses. Items 2 and 8 are also quite basic.

At some point during the discussion, you will find it useful to explain the notion of a continuum. Point out to the students that each individual response, and the total scores, represent a range of responses from the political right to the political left. Because the number of philosophical and policy issues covered in the survey is limited, the continuum represented by the final composite scores of the class is not so broad as it could conceivably be. However, the range probably comes close to capturing the full political spectrum for the United States as a whole.

After you have gone over the items, helping students to understand why a particular response is more to the right or to the left (because that is what the labels have come to mean), it is useful to ask students if they were surprised by their score and why.

Here is another suggestion about what to do after the survey has been completed. Place the students in ideologically alike groups. The grouping of students will be somewhat arbitrary, though the range of variation in scores for any one group probably should not be larger than four or five points. On the other hand, you probably don't want groups of fewer than three students. Once students are in groups, the class can be given a particular policy issue and asked to make recommendations. For instance, each group might recommend a U.S. defense policy, or an

72

employment policy, or a policy for dealing with some current or recent hot spot in the world. *Great Decisions,* published by the Foreign Policy Association, is a useful source for case studies dealing with international issues. (See Foreign Policy Association in the Resources section.)

A Humorous Perspective

In our work, we frequently encounter people from other nations. It is always enlightening and sometimes troubling to discover how differently they see us from how we see ourselves. Even though we are intellectually aware of the differences and why they exist, the experience is inevitably an emotional one. And it is not always the case that we see ourselves in a positive light while a person from another nation sees us in a negative one. For instance, the authors of this book have each had more than one experience where we were critical of an action taken by the U.S. government and the foreigner with whom we were talking was quite supportive of the action. But whatever the case, it is always helpful to remind ourselves that our perception of something is never shared by everyone else.

One interesting way to get students thinking about such differences in perspective is to have them collect political cartoons from the world's press. Most large magazine stores, bookstores, and libraries carry newspapers and magazines from around the world. One advantage of cartoons is that you don't necessarily have to be able to read the words to get the picture. A particularly useful source is *World Press Review* (see Resources section); each month's issue contains a feature entitled "The World in Cartoons."

One way to structure this activity is to select a series of major events involving the United States or major actions taken by the U.S. government. Put the students in groups and assign each group an event or action. The groups are then asked to collect a few cartoons from the U.S. press and several from other nations, all of which focus on the assigned event or action. What are the similarities and differences in how the United States is viewed or in how the event is depicted? Which tend to be most critical of the U.S. action? Which tend to be most supportive? Do they reflect a specific political orientation in the artist? What do the students know about the people, governments, and cultures of the other nations? Does this knowledge help explain the different viewpoints in the cartoons? How else would they explain the differences and the similarities?

International Interviews

Often international students and foreign visitors or residents in the community are a rich but untapped resource for our schools. Here's a way to help promote interaction between students and foreign nationals and to allow local students to learn about other parts of the world in the process.

The heart of the activity is to assign or allow students to select a country (one that has a national representative available in town). The students do some research on that country. Then they use the research as background for half-hour to hour-long interviews with the visitor from the country they have researched.

A good lead-in to pique student interest in beginning the research is to work as a group brainstorming the ideas, words, and statements that come to mind when class members first think of the country being studied. This activity will bring to light a number of stereotypes that students hold about the country. The first job of their research and later of their interviews is to ascertain the accuracy or inaccuracy of these stereotypes.

In order for the interview to proceed smoothly, it is a good idea to develop questions appropriate to the experiences of the person being interviewed. For instance, it would be appropriate to ask questions about current political events if the interviewee is someone who is politically active or follows politics closely. If the interviewee is a graduate student in engineering at a local university, then a different set of questions would be in order. In arranging for the interviews, not only do your students need to establish a place and time to meet, they also need to gain a sense of whether politics, education, family, religion, or sports would be good topics for the interview.

Here are a few sample questions to help your students get started:

About how many hours a week do you spend watching TV?

What is your favorite music group?

What newspaper do you read?

Do you have an allowance? How much?

What do you spend money on?

Does your family pray before meals?

Do you attend a church, mosque, or temple regularly?

What time do you usually eat your evening meal?

How much time do you spend on homework?

How do you spend a typical Saturday afternoon?

What is the first thing you do when you get home from school?

Who washes the dishes in your home?

How many adults live with you? Who are they?

Do you have pets? What kind?

In order to learn more about the values of other cultures, older and more sophisticated students may want to discuss such subjects as:

How do you define friendship or "a friend"?

What role do elderly people have in your family? In your society?

How do children display their independence from their parents and at what age?

What responsibilities does the wife/mother have in your family? Is her role typical of women in your society?

(The question above can be asked about father/husband also.)

How do young people pursue romantic relationships in preparation for marriage?

How much or how often do people touch each other when they are having a social conversation?

Who is more important in your society, the person who accomplishes a great deal or the person who comes from an old, respected family?

Do the members of your family like to be alone or do they spend most of their time with others?

What do you find most difficult to understand about Americans?

There are various educational settings that invite this activity. A geography class can do a global survey with reports from the interview given when timely. Students studying a particular region (for example, Latin America, China, Eastern Europe) can use the interviews to enhance their knowledge of the area. Interviews can also enrich language or history studies.

As Others See Us

Some years ago an American Visiting Fulbright Lecturer in Economics was asked the following questions by Indian university students in India. While some of the references may sound dated, the questions are typical of the kinds Americans still hear when overseas. For convenience, the questions are categorized under headings:

1. *Personal:* What is your party affiliation? What is your salary? Why do you allow your children to climb trees and risk hurting themselves? Why are American children so noisy? What occupations have you chosen for your children?

2. *Family in America:* Why are there so many divorces in America? It is said that American family life is breaking up fast; what efforts are being made to stabilize it? Some scholars have predicted the utter ruin of Western civilization because of the breakup of family life; what do you think? Are American men capable of choosing their mates wisely? What is the relationship between an American woman and her mother-in-law? Why do the English and Americans hate children?

3. *Sacrifice:* Are you making a sacrifice in giving aid to India? We know that when you grant aid to India, it helps maintain employment at home in the United States; why do you think that we should accept it if it is helpful to you to grant the aid?

4. *Political Economy:* Must Americans make war to prevent depression at home? How can America follow the path of peace when economic crises would follow any attempt to disarm? If senators are among America's richest people, don't their interests lie in war rather than peace? If most American senators are millionaires, how can social reform legislation ever be passed? What is the basis for the American attitude of opposition to communism? Why do American workers prefer capitalism? Why does America use aid to help unpopular [heads of government] suppress opposition at home?

5. *Race:* What is the position of black people? What language do they speak? Why does America allow racial discrimination while the communist countries have outlawed it? Could America have dropped the atom bomb on Europeans, or only on Asians? Why do Red Indians not have representation in Congress?

The attempt to understand an unfamiliar culture presents a number of problems. One of the most significant of these comes from applying our own cultural values and criteria when asking questions. You can learn a lot about another culture by paying close attention to the questions someone from that culture asks you. What can you tell about the values the Indian students held at the time they asked these questions? Can you make any generalizations about Indian life or Indian social and political perspectives from them? Which are the most accurate? Which are the most based on stereotypes?

Assign your students the task of finding a foreign student or visitor to interview them (i.e., to interview the students). Or invite someone in to interview the class as a whole (brief the interviewer on what you hope to achieve—perhaps showing him or her the Fulbright interview). Ask the students to note the questions that most surprised them and those that were most difficult to answer. How did they differ from those asked of the Fulbright professor in India? Why do they think they were different? What new insights about their own culture did they acquire from the interviews? What new insights about the interviewer's culture?

VALUING DIVERSITY

You don't have to spend much time with the news before it becomes apparent that the fear of people with different values and perspectives is one of the principal sources of discord and violence in the world. It is equally clear that the task before us is a lot more difficult than making people aware of our differences and similarities. What we need is to develop an appreciation for the value of diversity.

In this section we offer eleven activities which engage students positively in the appreciation of diversity. Because gaining this appreciation is something that people must experience, not just ponder intellectually, the majority of activities in this section explore the diversity in our immediate environment and focus on its importance in achieving goals we value. In fact, four of the first five activities ("Global Bingo," "What Can You Teach?," "Who Are the Kids?," and "How Many of You...?") utilize the diversity in the classroom as the basis for the learning.

Diversity is explored in a broader context in the "Cultural Geographic Study Tour" and "Global Theater," while the remaining activities in this section ("Calendars: Exploring Diversity," "A Day in the Life of...," "The Top News Stories," and "Whose News?") move the students on to an examination of the diversity in other parts of the world.

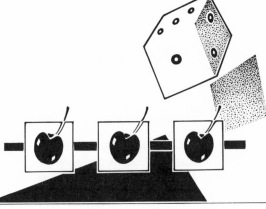

Global Bingo

This has become a particularly popular icebreaker at workshops and can be used for similar purposes in the classroom. When we play the game, we usually play "blackout bingo," that is, all the spaces have to be filled. A sample bingo card appears on the next page. You may make copies of this (one for each student) or devise your own set of questions. Some teachers use this activity as a way to review material for a test. For this purpose, you may wish to write the statements/questions yourself or have the students submit their ideas.

Begin the game by having each person write her or his name in the center space. Then the students move around trying to find someone who can provide the answer to the question in a particular space (such as naming 10 African countries) or who possesses the item in question (such as a bike made in another country) or who has done what the question asks. When a person has been found, that person writes his or her name in the space. Any person's name can appear on any given card only once. For instance, if Lisa signs her name in the "Who among us plays soccer?" space on my card, she can't sign any other spaces on my card. She can sign one space on each player's card.

You can play until one card is filled or until several or even all are filled, but you don't have to have a winner.

You can have a good follow-up discussion by asking the students what spaces were most difficult to fill, what surprised them in the game, and whether all of these global connections are good or bad news to them.

For this exercise, the instructor will, of course, need to adapt the questions to the age and/or makeup of the group.

Global Bingo

Who drives a foreign car?	Who has traveled overseas at least twice?	Who speaks and understands French or German?	Who has hosted or recently met someone from another country?	Who is wearing something made in a foreign country?
Who has relatives living in another country?	Who has traveled on an ocean liner?	Who has ever had a pen pal from another country?	Who has had his or her name in the newspaper?	Who among us plays soccer?
Who has taken a course about another part of the world?	Who has been to both Canada and Mexico?	PUT YOUR NAME HERE	Who makes good German food?	Who has a Spanish surname?
Who has lived in more than five states?	Who has a bike made in another country?	Who has a camera made in another country?	Who can name 10 countries in Africa?	Who can name the capital of Honduras?
Who speaks Spanish?	Who has parents who worked for the military?	Who comes from a family of seven or more children?	Who has gone to school in another country?	Who can name 6 countries in the Middle East?

Are All...Alike?

This activity was first called "Are All Indians Alike?" and was designed to counteract stereotyping of Native Americans and to help students become aware of the differences among Native-American groups. As the new title indicates, the activity can be used in many circumstances to help us reconsider our possible stereotypes and the accuracy of our perceptions.

Most people will admit that their images of another group do not apply to every person in that group. At least people will *say* they don't stereotype all people in a group. Yet some of us continue to act as if all people of Native-American (or African, Asian, Arab, etc.) descent are alike and should be treated alike. This activity gives students the opportunity to prove to themselves that the indigenous people of this country and the people of other cultures are not all alike but are members of diverse, culturally varied groups and that there are a great variety of mindsets and lifestyles among them.

This exercise also offers a wonderful opportunity to distinguish between and among

1. shared values, behaviors, and other cultural characteristics;

2. stereotypes (oversimplified identification of easily observed cultural characteristics used to speed up the process of sorting and classifying perceptions); and

3. negative stereotypes (a complex defensive psychological mechanism which enables people to allocate blame for the ills of the world to groups other than their own and frees them from the arduous task of perceiving and communicating accurately across cultural differences).

Students work in groups of two to four persons. Their assignment is to collect information and make a presentation to the entire class to prove that Native Americans (or Africans, Asians, Arabs, etc.) are *not* all alike. Allow one or two class periods for research and one or two for brief presentations and discussion. Students should be encouraged to use both the school library and home and community sources for their research.

Here is the step-by-step process:

1. Ask students if they can describe common characteristics of the people under study. Ask if they are alike and, if so, in what ways.

2. Tell the students that you would like them, for the time being, to work under the assumption that the people they are studying are more different than alike. Tell the students that their task is to try to prove this assumption.

3. Have students form working groups of two to four persons. Give them two days in class and outside to collect their information.

4. Have each group choose a person who will present the results to the class. (In one of George's eighth-grade social studies classes where students were proving that not all Arabs are alike, one group brought in an Arab to prove their point.)

5. Display around the classroom the materials that have been collected.

6. Have each student write a paragraph containing at least two statements that illustrate that not all...are alike, or ask students to write a short essay about what most surprised them in their research.

What Can You Teach?

This is another good icebreaker for the classroom, a workshop, or the first staff meeting of the year.

Each person is given a small slip of paper and writes on it something she or he can teach, for example, making paper trees, baking bread, *t'ai chi,* or whatever. The slips of paper are collected and placed in a basket or in some other container from which they can be drawn. Each person draws one slip and, after all the slips have been distributed, goes around the room trying to find the author of the slip he or she is holding. After everyone has identified a "teacher," each takes a turn introducing his or her teacher to the group.

Although we typically use this activity simply as an icebreaker, it could be used to introduce a discussion of what it means to be a teacher. Are we all teachers and learners? This activity offers an excellent opportunity for young people to see themselves as active authorities, as teachers, and not just as uninformed learners. Before beginning, the students might find helpful some class discussion about the kinds of things they have the ability to teach, since some may not consider their personal skills as something one normally teaches. But with a suggestion or two from you, it should be easy for them to come up with something. This activity can be made more focused by asking the students what they have to share with or teach the group with regard to the environment, or safety in the community, or dealing with foreigners or others who are culturally different.

Who Are the Kids?

Here is a straightforward way to gain some insights into your students. As many of us have learned the hard way, you have to begin with your students as they are: with what they know, don't know, feel, believe, and so on. It does no good to begin with where you hoped, or mistakenly thought, they were. And it's boring for them when you take them over ground they've covered too many times before or help them dispel mistaken ideas they never held in the first place.

The value of the approach here is its simplicity and directness. But its directness can also be its drawback. Students may balk at saying very much about themselves that is revealing. That is why we have included other activities in this book which have the same purpose but are not quite so obvious. We have found that this approach will work with many students and is always worth trying. Your experience will probably tell you which of the questions listed on page 93 are most likely to elicit honest responses. If you are not sure, try anyway—we are all learners.

Basically what you do is ask students to answer some questions, like those listed (but adapted to the age of your class), about themselves so that you can know them better as you begin your work together. The questions can be posed in several ways. Sometimes they are reproduced and handed out to the students, who bring back their responses the next day or write them out in class.

What we prefer is to read each question aloud and have the students write their responses immediately. When we do this at the beginning of a class or workshop, we are only trying to get a general feel for the group, so we don't require them to put their names on their answer sheets.

A suggestion: Before giving the questions to the students, summarize what you think are the principal kinds of responses they will make. This is a good test of what your own images and stereotypes of the kids are.

According to *World Almanac's* twelfth annual poll (published in the 1992 edition) of U.S. students in grades 8 to 12, the top ten heroes of American teenagers for 1991 were: H. Norman Schwarzkopf, Julia Roberts, George Bush, Michael Jordan, Barbara Bush, Mariah Carey, Kevin Costner, Oprah Winfrey, Madonna, Paula Abdul, and Sandra Day O'Connor (tied for tenth). You might want to compare your classes' heroes with those in the *Almanac*.

Who Are the Kids?

1. Have you lived in this town (city) all your life?

2. Have you ever lived outside the United States?

3. What are the four most important things in life for you?

4. Who are your three top heroes?

5. Who is the leader of Russia?

6. What does the term "U2" refer to (a spy plane or Irish rock group)?

7. Who is the U.S. Secretary of State?

8. What are your three favorite TV shows?

9. What are the five most important world problems today?

10. What are the five most important problems in this country today?

11. What magazines, if any, do you read on a regular basis?

12. Name two things that really make you mad.

13. Name two things that make you sad.

14. What are the three worst things that could happen to you?

15. What is the name of the principal of this school?

16. What is the name of the mayor of this town (city)?

17. What was the Rio Summit?

18. Approximately how many people are there in the world?

19. Do you think drugs should be legalized?

20. Do you think men are naturally smarter in math and science than women?

How Many of You...?

Another good way to learn about your students—a way that's less threatening than direct questions to individuals—is to ask "how many of you..." questions. For example:

How many of you are an only child?

How many of you have more than three siblings, more than four, more than five, and so forth?

How many of you are left-handed?

How many of you live in single-parent homes?

How many of you like to take photographs? Play the piano? Sing? Dance?

How many of you have a job after school?

How many wish you were richer?

How many have been seriously ill in the past five years?

This kind of activity can be especially effective in very mixed groups, ones including people from differing nations and cultures. After a few questions students will begin to notice and feel more comfortable with both their similarities and differences. And they may note some ethnic trends in the responses.

This activity can also be useful in alerting the teacher or discussion leader to the presence of students with international experience, who constitute a special resource for global education. To elicit such information ask questions such as:

How many of you know someone who has lived in (insert the name of a country you are about to study)?

How many of you have lived in another country?

How many of you have a friend from a different national, cultural, or racial background than your own?

How many of you would like to have such a friend?

How many of you would like to live for a while in a foreign country?

Mainstream Americans are becoming more ethnically conscious than they were during the melting pot era and are recognizing the importance of their ethnic roots. Identifying those feelings can create a strong connection between the students and things international and cross-cultural. So you might ask:

How many of you have a strong heritage from another country in your family background?

How many of you speak a foreign language?

How many of you have relatives born in a foreign country?

This is also a good activity for raising awareness of the personal significance of global issues about to be studied. For instance:

How many of you know someone who lives on the streets?

How many of you have family members who have served in a war?

How many of you have family members or friends who are having trouble finding work?

How many of you know of someone who uses the drugs being dealt in our city?

Often, once this activity is started, students want to join in offering questions of their own. Their questions will also teach you a great deal about who they are and what concerns them.

One caution in using this activity. Especially if you work in a politicized school system, think carefully about the questions you choose to ask and discard or word carefully the ones that are most apt to cause complaint. Usually those are the ones dealing with religion and money (which we have avoided here).

Calendars: Exploring Diversity

For exploring such global themes as diversity and multiple perspectives, calendars, with their wide variety of shapes, sizes, illustrations, themes, and formats, are an excellent, plentiful, and readily available resource. We recommend seeking out the many wonderful calendars with international photos, such as UNICEF's, Paintings from Latin America, Animals around the World, and so on.

To help students experience and understand the value of multiple perspectives, divide them into trios or quartets. Give each group several calendars. The calendars should be ones that show a different picture as each month is displayed. Have each student in each group privately select a favorite and least favorite picture and then discuss the choice and the reasons for it with the rest of the group. After everyone has had a chance to do that, reassemble the class and ask if the students in each group all chose the same pictures and if they believe there were right or wrong choices. (We hope the answers will be no.) Then discuss with them what the exercise taught them about people's opinions and how subjective they are.

Once you're ready to take the calendars apart, there are other exercises you can try. Here's one. Have students select a picture and then get together with four or five other students who have pictures that they agree illustrate a common theme or category (e.g., water, children, nature, conflict). Then have them regroup to create new themes or categories.

Here's another possibility. Have each student select a picture or series of pictures as a focus for a story or poem.

And finally, one more. Have students design their own calendar. They could collect information and/or pictures from holidays, other countries, or special days with international significance (e.g., the founding of the United Nations, Venezuelan Independence Day, the Chinese New Year) from as many sources as possible and make one master calendar full of information. This could be an ongoing class activity. Or they could collect pictures from all over the world that express a common theme.

A Day in the Life of...

Here's an idea that will encourage students to observe what is occurring around them and to compare their observations about life.

Japan, Israel, Australia, the United States, the former Soviet Union, Canada, and Spain participated in a unique photographic event. On one single day, famous photographers spread across each nation to try to capture part of the essence of the people. The results are available in book form for each country.

In the United States, the task was to compile "a visual time capsule" of everyday life. The result was more than 200,000 images of the United States, all taken during the twenty-four hours of an otherwise ordinary Friday in May, 1986. The pictures in the book were selected from these 200,000. Here are some activities using these books (see below for publisher information).

Have the students guess what kinds of pictures they are most likely to see in the book they (or you) choose to work with. Then have them check the book to see how many of their guesses are correct. A follow-up discussion can focus on what they saw in the book that they didn't expect to see and why they were surprised.

Based on what they observe in the pictures, have each student write fifteen statements about the country and then share their statements. Which statements are repeated most often? Which statements can be made as generalizations for the whole country? Which can't and why? What do they think it would *feel* like to live in that country?

Using news photos and stories, have students collect an hour in the life of America and then compare that to the same hour in the life of the world.

As a class project, the students can create a day in the life of their own community and then consider what someone from one of the countries covered by the books would think about it. They could base this analysis on the comparisons between the day in their community and the days depicted in the published books.

> **Note:** The book on Israel is titled *The Israelis: Photographs of a Day in May* (published in the U.K.). All the others are titled *A Day in the Life of...*, San Fran-

cisco: Collins Publishers. Publication dates are as follows: America, 1986; Australia, 1982; Canada, 1984; China, 1989; Ireland, 1991; Italy, 1990; Japan, 1985; Soviet Union, 1987; Spain, 1988.

Cultural Geographic Study Tour

This activity was designed by our very good friends, Melissa Aronson and Ida Bowers. Both are university teachers, one in a school of education, the other in a department of geography. Both previously have taught in public schools at the secondary level.

The "study tour" was created as a way to provide students with an increased understanding of basic geographic concepts and some notion of the ways a geographer looks at the world. Most importantly, the activity helps students develop their observation skills and helps them see that in using these skills they, not text or other external "authorities," are ultimately the most important source of information about and vehicle for understanding the world."

Hand your students the list of questions which follows and tell them to go find the answers. They can do this individually, though we recommend that they conduct their research in groups of twos or threes. The research will take a good eight hours or so. If you don't want them to spend that amount of time, you can shorten the exercise by cutting down the number of questions assigned to each group.

The geographic area of this study tour is the school district. Of course, it could easily be modified to the town, city, or county.

As a final classroom activity to help tie the elements of the research together, have the students sketch the physical setting of the district, being sure to indicate their path of travel on the study tour.

When the students have completed their study tour and their sketches, guide a discussion around three broad questions:

> What new discoveries did you make about the district and the community?

> What conclusions have you come to about the area?

> What did you learn about your district's and community's international connections?

Cultural Geographic Study Tour

1. What are the district boundaries? Why are they where they are? What is on your district's side of the boundary? What is on the other side?

2. What cultural groups are represented? Where did they come from? When? What were the factors that drove them from their homeland (push factors) and what factors attracted them to their new home (pull factors)?

3. Where do different cultural groups come in contact with each other? Where do people come in contact mostly with their own cultural group?

4. When was the community your district is part of founded? By whom? Why?

5. What are the major roads? Where do they go? Are new roads in the planning or construction stage? What will be the impact on the district?

6. What are the principal economic activities of the district? What are its major imports and exports?

7. What parks and recreation areas exist in the district? Who uses them?

8. How has the area changed over the last 10-25 years? What traces on the landscape can you see of the past? What do you think the area will look like in 10 years; what hints of the future can you see?

9. Select a cemetery and walk through it. What did you discover?

10. What churches exist? Who belongs? Are they growing, stable, or shrinking?

11. What other institutions do you find in the district that inform you about who the students are?

12. How is your community related to other parts of the region?

The Top News Stories

At the beginning of each calendar year, a variety of analyses of what was most significant in the previous year is offered to the public. The Associated Press has long published a list of the 10 top news stories. Often, local papers, especially the large city papers, will print their own lists. Television commentators discuss the subject at length. And now, each February, *World Press Review* lists the 10 top news stories as seen by editors around the world. The lists provide excellent opportunities to examine a variety of perspectives on international issues. Here are some things you might do.

Have students, either individually or in small groups, compare and discuss the lists. The students might take the perspective of the reporters or editors of a single list, explaining the importance of the stories they chose.

Ask the students to identify which stories appear most often on the lists. Are these stories important to everyone for the same reasons or do they have a different significance in different parts of the world?

Ask the students if they see any bias in those who selected each of the lists. Have them share their perceptions as to the specific foreign policy goals or national priorities that determine how each journalist or editor viewed the top stories of the year.

The lists can be used with maps. Have the students note on a world map where the stories occurred and/or originated. Which countries were the source of the most news? Which stories affected more than one country?

Students could make their own lists. They don't have to confine themselves to the stories selected by others. Each month they could revise their choices of stories from the previous month and update their list to include more recent news events. Separate lists for international, national, state, local, and school news could be compiled.

Whose News?

For most of us, our sources for learning about what goes on in the world are local or national newspapers, magazines, television, and radio. No matter how objective we or they try to be, we cannot escape the fact that they express a viewpoint of people who live and work in the United States. To improve critical thinking as well as to heighten our consciousness of the fact that our own perspective on any given subject is only one of many reasonable perspectives on it, it is useful to have students read articles from newspapers and magazines written in other countries. Here are some ways to go about doing this.

At the high school level, you can involve students who are taking foreign language courses. Obtain copies of newspapers and/or magazines from French-, Russian-, Spanish-, Japanese-, and German-speaking countries (and any other languages which are taught at your school) which include stories on the same topic. Students from each language course can explain the story or translate it into English. Then engage the class in a discussion of the variations in point of view exhibited in the articles. How differently is the same story treated? How do you account for the differences?

An alternative to this is to obtain copies of newspapers from different countries, including the United States, published on the same day. Look for stories dealing with international issues or events. Do the papers deal with the same events and issues? In what ways do they differ? When different papers deal with the same events, do they treat those events similarly? How?

Another approach is to use *World Press Review.* Each month's edition carries news stories from around the world. Divide students into groups of three or four and give each group one or two editions. Ask them to find similarities and differences in the way the stories are treated. Do they find that stories from different countries dealing with the same issue vary greatly? How?

Global Theater

Today most schools and universities have groups of students from many different nations and cultures. This activity, which was created by John C. Condon, will make students, especially those of the dominant culture, more aware of both the similarities and differences among the cultures represented.

The activity requires 3 to 5 people of a single culture who speak a different language or have a strong dialect that differs from that of most of the class and who are willing to perform in a brief skit. These people could be international students or African, Hispanic, Asian, or Native American students. The role-play group should include at least one male and one female. If the common culture of the role players isn't distinguished by language or dialect, the role play can be done in pantomime.

The group is asked to enact a brief (3-8 minutes) scene depicting some relatively simple event which is part of their everyday lives and which ideally contains actions or interactions especially characteristic of their culture or ethnic group.

When the skit is completed, the class (but *not* the role players) discusses the role play, trying to determine just what happened and exploring any differences between how the people in the skit behaved and how people in their own family, culture, or ethnic group would behave under similar circumstances.

At first the role players are not allowed to say anything. After 5 or 10 minutes, they are allowed to answer questions and reveal what was happening—but only in response to the questions.

This part of the activity is followed by a free-ranging discussion among students, role players, and instructor. Even the simplest skit can produce a wonderful discussion of how people behave and how their behavior is perceived, especially across cultural lines.

LIVING RESPONSIBLY WITH OTHERS

While we believe that all six of our themes are closely related, the themes of this and the previous two sections are inextricably linked, because it is impossible to live responsibly in this world without being aware of one's own values and perspectives and without valuing diversity. Thus the activities of section two focus students' attention on their own values and perspectives, while section three moves to a consideration of the diversity around us and the value of that diversity in building healthy, stimulating, and strong communities.

In this section, we provide thirteen activities which not only engage students in the process of trying to interact responsibly and productively with others, but also raise fundamental questions about how certain social structures can create obstacles to responsible interaction. One of the most difficult dilemmas we all face in attempting to act morally is the conflict between individual needs and the common good. Because we feel this dilemma is so central to the notion of living responsibly with others—or building community—it is a focus of many of the activities in this section, such as "Human Rights," "Arms and Resources," and "In an Ideal World."

Most of the activities in this section are designed to help equip students with the skills to deal with others in difficult situations. This is particularly true with "Global Deadlines," "The Golden Rule," and "Temperature Check." Other activities, such as "History That Counts," "Does Excellence Mean Winning?," and "Rich and Poor," provide techniques for exploring some of the social structures which may impede cooperative and productive relations. All the activities in this section will contribute to building skills and attitudes for living in the world community.

Global Deadlines

There are lots of conditions we all would like to see corrected: war, hunger, pollution, job uncertainty, terrorism. But we also know that no individual, community group, government, or private agency can tackle all the problems at once. Everyone has to set priorities before effective action can be taken. But how? On what basis do we decide that significant effort should be directed toward one problem rather than another? This is an activity that will get students thinking about the question of priorities.

Here is a list of problems:

1. Depletion of the ozone layer

2. Rapid population growth

3. Proliferation of nuclear weapons

4. Possible extinction of the whales

5. Tropical deforestation

6. Starvation of large numbers of people

7. Imbalances in the global economy

8. Pollution of rivers and streams

9. Growing numbers of refugees and homeless

Each student should be given this list and told that he or she has 2 minutes to rank-order these problems according to the priority with which they should receive attention, if the student could set the international political agenda. In other words, which item on this list merits the most immediate attention, which would come next, and so on? They are not necessarily ranking the problems in terms of their gravity, but in terms of which problem they believe should be targeted first. Their reasons for their rankings will vary and these differences then become the basis for the discussion at the end of the exercise.

After the students have completed their rankings, they should be grouped based on their first choice. All those who thought deforestation was the problem to tackle first would be one group, those who listed refugees and homeless first would be another, and so forth. Each group is then given 15 minutes to compose a brief (1-3 minutes) presentation supporting the correctness of its choice. We usually suggest that they select the 3 most compelling arguments in favor of their position.

Following the presentations, there are several topics worth discussing. You might begin by asking if anyone's mind has been changed and why. You can also ask what sorts of information they believe they would need to improve their case and where they think they might get the information. Obviously, this can become the basis of individual or group research projects, with a final set of presentations at the end of the research. At some point, you may want to list and discuss the various reasons given for each group's choice.

Finally, if the question hasn't emerged in the discussion, ask if it's important for everyone to have the same priorities. We find students are comforted and empowered by the realization that they don't have to deal with all the world's problems. The people who see things differently are, in fact, helping one another to see the whole picture.

In-School World Tour

If you live near a college or university with a significant international student population, here's a great way to provide your students with an intercultural exchange experience. This admittedly ambitious activity is one of the best examples of school, community, and university collaboration we've heard of. The model was designed by Pat Tolmie and her colleagues at Winona State University in Minnesota.

The bare bones of the activity are as follows:

- An entire grade school agrees to stage a "world tour" day.

- The university collects small groups of its students from 5 or 6 different countries.

- The students plan ways to share experiences and information about their countries using costume, art, music, dances, lectures, artifacts, food, language instruction, or any other means they think of.

- Local education students coach the international students about what to expect in U.S. schools. (Often the norms and practices are very different from those in their home countries.)

- On the appointed day, various rooms in the school become different nations.

- Classes move from country to country, experiencing each and getting a passport stamped in each place.

- The day ends with a grand, and always moving, international show with music, processions, and presentation of flags.

We hope many people will try this delightful idea, but before you do, we suggest that you contact Pat Tolmie for more detailed advice. Her address is: Gildemeister 140, PO Box 5838, Winona, MN 55987-5838.

The Golden Rule

A fundamental guide to moral behavior familiar to Christians is the Golden Rule. A fascinating fact about this rule is that it is found in most of the world's commonly practiced religions, though expressed in different ways. On the following page we have listed eight versions of the Golden Rule. Here are some suggestions for what you can do with the list.

At the beginning of each school year, many teachers engage their students in a conversation to develop rules for the class. The process will be more effective if teachers provide a few examples of the sorts of things they have in mind. Giving students a copy of the different ways of stating the Golden Rule can be one very useful example.

Whether done in the context of forming class rules or just as a general discussion of social rules and culture, it is intriguing to speculate as to why the Golden Rule is so culturally widespread. If the students do not suggest it, you might propose the possibility that it is because the desire to be respected and to be treated fairly is fundamental in human beings. It is also worth speculating about whether the Golden Rule is the most basic of social rules. Judaism, Confucianism, Christianity, and Brahmanism, for instance, all indicate this to be the case.

If you are teaching a course on world history, an early discussion of the ubiquity of the Golden Rule will aid in the search for other cultural constants. In this context you might want to refer to the provocative work of Joseph Campbell. Although much of his published work is too complex for most precollege students, the series of televised interviews on PBS with Bill Moyers, *The Power of Myth,* and the companion book of the same title, can be useful classroom resources. Campbell suggests a number of social rules and norms that are found frequently throughout time and among a variety of cultures.

The Golden Rule

Christianity: "All things whatsoever ye would that others should do to you, do ye even so to them, for this is in the Law and the Prophets."
                              —Matthew

Judaism: "What is hateful to you, do not to another. That is the entire law, all the rest is commentary."
                              —Talmud

Islam: "No one of you is a believer until he desires for his brother that which he desires for himself."
                              —Sunnah

Confucianism: "Is there one maxim which ought to be acted upon throughout one's whole life? Surely, it is the maxim of loving kindness. Do not unto others what you would not have them do unto you."
                              —Analects

Buddhism: "Hurt not others in ways that you yourself would find hurtful."
                              —Udana Varga

Brahmanism: "This is the sum of duty: do naught unto others which would cause you pain if done to you."
                              —*Mahabharata*

Taoism: "Regard your neighbor's gain as your own gain, and your neighbor's loss as your own loss."
                              —T'ai Shang Kan Ying P'ien

Zoroastrianism: "That nature alone is good which refrains from doing unto another whatsoever is not good for itself."
                              —Dadistan I. Dinik

116

Culture and Values

Here's an excellent tool for pursuing values clarification and building cross-cultural awareness. The activity works best in groups where a variety of national, cultural, or ethnic groups are represented, though any group of people brings great diversity of values with them. The basic concept behind this exercise is that it brings to the surface assumptions and values which govern our behavior but which lie largely out of awareness. When people in this kind of benign learning environment confront differences in fundamental and deeply held values, they are able to discuss and rationalize their differences without conflict. They can also, if they are ready, come to respect and even appreciate the differing values and value systems they encounter.

The form on the following page calls for each student to rank-order the values, according to his or her own beliefs, in the first column to the right, the one headed "self." The values will be ranked from 1 (the top priority) to 19 (the bottom priority).

Then students are gathered into small groups of four to six to compare their rankings and to see if they can agree upon rankings as a group. Here it is best to narrow the focus to the top three or four values and the bottom three or four. (It is too cumbersome to debate all nineteen.)

Finally, the rankings are revealed to the whole group, compared, and discussed.

As a variation, the students can be asked to give what they think would be the rankings of a person from one or two other culture groups which are represented among the students. The columns headed "other" are to be used for these other rankings.

This exercise tends to produce deep probing of beliefs among the participants and enables the instructor to explore with them the value differences that exist between cultures and the implications of these differences for intercultural communication and cross-cultural human relations.

Value Selection Form

	SELF	OTHER	OTHER
1. A Comfortable Life			
2. An Exciting Life			
3. A Sense of Accomplishment			
4. A World at Peace			
5. A World of Beauty			
6. Equality			
7. Family Unity and Security			
8. Freedom			
9. Happiness			
10. Inner Harmony			
11. Mature Love			
12. National Security			
13. Pleasure			
14. Religious Principles			
15. Self-Respect			
16. Social Recognition			
17. True Friendship			
18. Wisdom			
19. Moral Life			

118

Human Rights

Any teacher or parent knows that youngsters can get obsessed with their right to do this and their right to do that. While this passion for their rights can be annoying, it also offers an excellent opportunity to engage students in serious discussion about international human rights. Here are some things you can do.

Provide your students with copies of the Universal Declaration of Human Rights. This document was adopted by the United Nations in 1948 and represents at least a rhetorical international consensus on what ought to constitute human rights.

Tell the students that they will be debating a revision of the document in which only 5 (or 7 or 10 or whatever) of the 30 articles will be retained. Which 5 do they want to keep? Why? Each student can represent his or her own position, or students can be placed in groups with each group presenting its position. The groupings can be assigned randomly or you can have the students take the Political Values Survey and assign them to ideologically alike groups. It is interesting to observe and examine the differences between what the more conservative and the more liberal students choose as the most important rights.

An alternative exercise is to ask the students to compose their own Global Bill of Rights and then compare theirs with the Universal Declaration. Which rights appear in both? Which appear only in the United Nations' document? Which appear only in the students' version? Is there any pattern to the differences? How would you explain the differences?

Rather than working with the Universal Declaration, your students might be more engaged by working with the Declaration of the Rights of the Child, ratified by the United Nations in 1959. Either of the two activities described above will work well with this document.

The September 1985 issue of *Social Education* (49, 6) contains a particularly helpful article by Lillian Genser, "Children's Rights and Responsibilities: A Teaching Unit for the Elementary Grades."* The article includes an annotated version of the Declaration of the Rights of the Child.

Social Education. 3501 Newark St., N.W., Washington DC 20016.

Over the past few decades, other international rights documents have been adopted by the United Nations. These include the International Covenant on Economic, Social, and Cultural Rights, the International Covenant on Civil and Political Rights, and the Convention on the Elimination of Discrimination against Women. From these documents 3 broad categories of rights emerge. Below we list these categories with examples of the kinds of rights found in each category. This list can be helpful in the examination of rights we are suggesting in the activities above.

120

Types of Human Rights

A. Economic, Social, and Cultural Rights

Right to work

Right to just conditions of work

Trade union rights and right to strike

Right to secure living conditions

Right of families, mothers, and children to protection

Right to food, clothing, and housing

Right to physical and mental health

Right to education

Right to enjoy the benefits of scientific progress

Right of authors to benefit from their scientific, literary, or artistic production (intellectual property rights)

B. Civil and Political Rights

Right to live

Freedom from torture

Freedom from slavery

Freedom of conscience and religion

Freedom of opinion and expression

Freedom from arbitrary arrest or detention

Right to humane treatment under detention

Freedom from imprisonment for debt

Freedom of movement and residence

Protection of aliens from expulsion

Right to a fair trial

Right to privacy

Freedom of assembly

Freedom of association

Right to marry

Rights of children

Right to vote

Right to hold political office

Right to equal protection of the law

C. Rights of Peoples and Minorities

Right of peoples to self-determination

Right of peoples to permanent sovereignty over natural resources

Rights of ethnic, religious, and linguistic minorities

Here are some additional questions to have your students discuss. Which kinds of rights are contained in the Bill of Rights of the U.S. Constitution? Which kinds of rights are not found in the U.S. Constitution? How would you explain this? Should the U.S. Constitution contain these other rights?

History That Counts

We have found this activity useful for exploring with the students those experiences that have made, or are making, them conscious of themselves as part of the larger world. What we do is simply to engage the students in a period of sharing memories of significant social and political events of the past. Specifically we ask them what news events they remember most vividly and why.

Here's what happened in one high school workshop. When we described our memories, they were, of course, the old standbys—the Berlin Wall, the assassinations of the sixties, the Bay of Pigs, civil rights milestones, events from the Vietnam era, Watergate. The students' memories were interesting in their difference and were sometimes surprising. For example, many of them mentioned the space shuttle disaster, which actually wasn't so surprising; but we weren't expecting them to mention the killing of John Lennon or the boycotting of the Summer Olympics of 1980 and 1984—but many did.

In our experience, this sort of discussion will bring up any number of issues about what it means to live responsibly today, because when thinking of significant memories, students will discover that most of them go back to times when they were struck by the discrepancy between what they thought the world ought to be and what it was. For instance, when discussing the Olympics, the students raised questions ranging from terrorism to global economic inequities to individualism versus the state. In all cases, the conversation revolved around the gap between what the students thought should be and what was.

A follow-up to this would be to move the conversation to a discussion of other discrepancies they see that bother them. From this you can put together a list of topics for further exploration in future class discussions, essays, stories and poems, reports, or research projects.

More or Less

This is a very simple activity that works well in prompting people to talk about the state of the world and about perspective consciousness. Have the students bring in pictures of things that they believe we need more of and things they believe we need less of in today's world.

Ask them to hang the pictures on a bulletin board and explain their choices. Is this a picture of something we need more or less of? Why?

Here is another thing you can do. Divide the class into groups of three or four. Distribute the pictures so that each group has pictures other than those selected by themselves. As a group, they should decide whether the picture represents something we need more or less of in the world today. After the group has decided, the student who initially brought the picture can explain his or her choice and compare it to the group's.

As a follow-up, ask students, based on the pictures they chose, to make a statement about their preferred state of the world. For example, a student might say, "My choices indicate that I want a more peaceful world," or "...a less polluted world," or "...a more automated world." Note and discuss any trends that emerge.

You can make the assignment more specific by having the students bring in things we need more or less of if we are to have a more secure world or a more prosperous world; or things we need more or less of if we are to improve the global ecology, and so forth.

The 3-minute, unnarrated 16mm film *More* can be used with this activity. It would be a great motivator to help students find their own pictures and also makes a thought-provoking statement about consumption. The film was originally distributed by Macmillan Films. It is now available from: Education Department, Films, Inc., 5547 N. Ravenswood Ave., Chicago, IL 60640-1199.

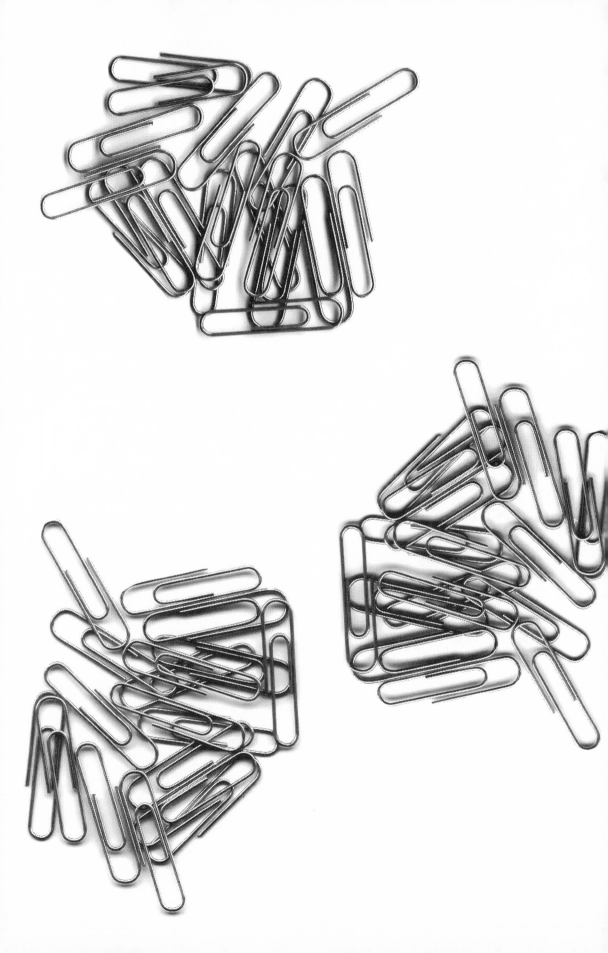

Arms and Resources

This simulation is effective in modeling for students the conflicts leaders face in trying to meet both the military and social needs of a country. It was adapted from the project, Sociological Resources for the Social Studies. The game is easy to play in 30-45 minutes and uses only paper clips. The entire class can participate because the game is played between pairs of students. Here is how it works.

Give each student 20 paper clips. These clips are their resources. Then pair up the students. Read the following instructions to the students:

1. The object of the game is to end up with as large a **Resources** pile as possible. Anyone with 15 or more clips at the end of the game is a winner.

2. To start, place all 20 of your clips in one pile. This is your Resources pile.

3. I will announce the beginning and end of each round. You will have to make decisions quickly because the round will be short.

4. During each round you have to decide to do one of the following:
    a. move 1 clip from Resources to another pile which is your **Arms** pile, or
    b. move 1 clip from Arms (if you have any) to Resources, or
    c. leave things as they are.

5. Be sure to conceal both your Resources and your Arms piles so that your opponent cannot see them.

6. After a very brief period of time (about 30 seconds or so), I will announce that the round has ended. At this time, I will ask if there are any **Attacks**. To Attack your opponent, you must have at least 4 clips in your Arms pile. If you want to Attack, then raise your hand when I ask if there are any Attacks. If you Attack, then a referee will come and count your

Arms clips and your opponent's Arms clips, and tell you if the battle was decisive. The battle will be determined in the same way if both opponents Attack at the same time. (At this point, you should select 1 or 2 referees or you may prefer to referee yourselves.)

7. Here is how you will know the outcome of the Attack.

   a. A decisive battle occurs when one player leads by 4 or more Arms clips, that is, when one player has at least 4 more clips in his or her Arms pile than the other player. When this happens, 6 clips will be taken from the loser's Resources pile and given to the winner's Resources pile. If the loser has less than 6 clips (in the Resources pile), then all that he or she does have will be taken.

   b. An indecisive battle occurs if Arms piles are within 3 clips of each other. In this case, no Resources are moved.

   c. As a result of *any* Attack, *all* Arms clips of both players are destroyed and will be permanently removed by the referee.

8. Your final score is determined by counting the number of clips in your Resources pile after all rounds are completed. (You can announce the number of rounds that will be played. You may do as many as you want. The upper limit is 20—because the players each have 20 clips and move 1 clip per round; 10 rounds is usually adequate, however.)

Play should move quickly so that students are quite absorbed in the action and their decisions. Some will be eliminated; they must then simply wait as the game plays out, and there's much to be learned from that experience.

After the simulation has been completed, discuss the experience. We find it useful to move away from the "game structure" and into a circle for this discussion. This helps the students shift from a competitive game atmosphere to one of sharing and conversation.

Here are some suggestions for questions you might ask during the discussion.

- How do you feel about the game?

- How did it feel to be attacked?

- How did it feel to be a loser? To be a winner?

- Did anyone cheat and move more than 1 clip at a time? If not, did you ever think about cheating?

- What do the Resources clips represent in the real world?

- How is this game similar to the real world? How is it different?

- Did you learn anything from the game that is relevant to the real world? How or why?

The discussion should prompt the participants to examine their thinking, the reasons for the choices they made, and the consequences. Through exercises such as this, we hope that young people can learn to think carefully enough to avoid making irrevocable mistakes both for themselves and the world.

Does Excellence Mean Winning?

A lot of the games we participate in at school, home, or camp teach us that being our best can only be accomplished at the expense of others. We end up confusing excellence with winning.

Recently, an "anti–war-toy brochure" was published which included comments from students who were asked to describe toys that made them feel warlike. One student's response was fascinating because the war toy he liked least was the game Monopoly. He said: "Monopoly makes me feel greedy and want everything for myself. I don't care what the other person gets." To be his best at the game, he had to be the winner and the others the losers.

One way to explore this issue with your students is to ask them what kinds of games they like to play. Outside of class, by yourself, analyze these games—what are the students learning from the rules and procedures? Are the games lifelike? If students haven't mentioned it, ask in what ways the games reflect real events in their lives, both locally and globally. Then have students discuss what they like and dislike about the games they have listed and share your observations with them. Do most prefer games they can win? Suggest that students try to redesign some of their games so that nobody loses. Which of the redesigned games would still be fun? Which wouldn't?

Here is another idea. To help students think about excellence as an idea separate from winning, have students write a short essay on the topic, "I Know I'm Doing My Best When...is." Or, somewhat more specifically, "I Know I'm Doing My Best at...when...."

And here is one more suggestion. Explore, either with your students or faculty colleagues, the way your school encourages excellence. Do all the contests require many more losers than winners? Are there contests in which everyone is or can be a winner? How do the students feel about the school contests? If most have few winners and lots of losers, could they be redesigned?

In an Ideal World

The White House Conference on Aging, held in Washington, D.C. in 1981, produced a number of statements that described living conditions of older people in an ideal world. Next to each of the statements of the ideal was a description of actual conditions today. The format is an excellent one for identifying what we should be striving for and how far we have to go to get there. The exercise forces us to evaluate current conditions and explore why they exist and then to consider what the ideal conditions ought to be and why.

We have listed a few of the statements from the Conference report. Have the students add several more statements about living conditions of the elderly and then, if you can, obtain a copy of the report, and let them compare their statements with the report. Or you can use this format for almost any other topic. It would be especially interesting to have them do a report on children—in their state, in the United States, in the world—or a report on peace, education, women, or refugees in the world. The Earth Summit, held in Brazil in the summer of 1992, is a virtual cornucopia of reports. Such reports can be very good small-group, cooperative-learning projects.

In an Ideal World	Today
Every older person would have enough income to pay for nutritious food, comfortable home, clothes, transportation, medical care, and participation in the total life of the community.	One-quarter of all older people live in households with income below the poverty level. The aged poor are now 20 percent of the total poor.
The health system would be organized to include preventive measures and early detection and treatment for even minor conditions.	The great majority must do without. The care they can get is either fragmented and lacking in continuity or is too costly.

In an Ideal World

Older people who never completed their education when they were young could do so if they chose.

Today

A fifth of the people 65 and older cannot read and write well enough to deal competently with the modern, complex world.

134

Rich and Poor

Here is a simple idea for discussion that will yield a wonderful breadth and intensity of feeling and insight. Ask the students why some people are rich and why some are poor.

As we have developed the process, we have found that it works best when using the following procedure. First, tell the students they are going to have a discussion about why some people are rich and some poor. Then tell them you want them to take a few moments to reflect on this question and to jot down a few of their thoughts. After a relatively brief period of time, randomly assign students to groups of four or five and ask them to brainstorm reasons why some people are rich and some poor. Give each group a couple of markers and a large sheet of paper so they can record their ideas.

After the groups have completed their lists, have each select one or two spokespersons. The spokespersons will go over the list with the class.

Next, open the discussion. This can be in the form of a general reaction to the ideas that have been generated, or you might ask the students to rank-order the reasons that have been offered from most to least important, or to categorize them into "very important," "important," and "only slightly important."

There will be disagreement. Some students will strongly reject the generalizations others give as reasons (e.g., people are lazy; businesses take exorbitant profits.)

After getting this kind of fix on wealth and poverty among people, shift the focus to countries. Why are some countries rich and some poor? Are there any similarities between wealth and poverty as they appear among people and as they appear among nations? What are the differences between wealthy nations and poor nations?

You can follow up this exercise by asking the students to do some research involving interviews with their parents to see if they come up with the same responses, or interviews with a number of rich people and a number of poor people. The research should also include studies by experts and government reports.

A different sort of research project is to have students select a poor country and describe the way its poverty is manifest, what its causes are, and what the people of that country should do about it.

Finally, students may want to talk about whether anything can or should be done about the situation. Is it inevitable that some people and/or nations will be wealthy and some poor? Are there poor people or nations who don't want to be poor? Can anything be done about that? Is there anything the students can do? Is there a downside to living in a wealthy country? An upside to living in a poor one?

Temperature Check

When we run workshops or student programs lasting more than 2 days, we begin each day with a "temperature check." This isn't an activity specifically designed for exploring global issues, but it is one of our basic techniques for encouraging people to practice communication and community building. The ability to see and work for the common good is a basic skill for a global citizen. Steve has used this same technique in the classroom, and we know many other teachers who use it in class and who have used it in workshops.

The purpose of a temperature check is to give every participant time and opportunity to say what's on his or her mind or in his or her heart. People can thank others for doing or saying something; they can express concerns; they can raise points of confusion. The temperature check is a sort of time-out which legitimizes a very personal discussion about what is going on, what people want to keep doing, and what they want changed.

When we do it, we provide 5 categories within which people can speak: appreciations, new information, puzzlements, concerns with recommendations, and hopes. "Appreciations" is the category to say how much you learned from Jane's presentation or how you appreciated Juan's willingness to share his personal experience or how good last night's supper was. The "new information" category permits announcements, the day's agenda, changes in scheduling, the due date for the paper, the time of the next exam. "Puzzlements" are questions you have for which you don't necessarily expect an answer, though you would like one. You're puzzled about a comment someone made yesterday or you are puzzled about the purposes of an assignment or you are puzzled about the meaning of life.

The "concerns with recommendations" category permits people to raise a question about or voice an objection to something. But, in order to keep things on a constructive note, any concern that is voiced must be accompanied by a suggestion as to how to remedy the problem, though it must be understood that the suggestion will not necessarily be followed. It may be beyond anyone's authority or ability to implement. It may be too costly; it may be unfair to too many others; someone else may come up with a better idea. But the person raising the concern must have given some thought not only to his or her problem but also to how it can be addressed. Temperature checks are not gripe sessions.

Finally, there is the "hopes" category. What would you like to see happen today? What would you like to see happen for the rest of the session, or the term? What do you hope won't happen again?

In our experience, people feel uncomfortable with the temperature check when it is first introduced. Frequently, the first day it is used, few people will speak and then only briefly. Usually by the second day, and almost invariably by the third, most people are beginning to get the feel of it and enjoy the relatively unstructured discussion. As should be clear, the utility of listing and explaining the 5 categories is that it helps keep the discussion constructive. Should the discussion begin to degenerate, you can remind the group of the categories.

The temperature check format is often so successful that lengthy and exciting discussions are generated, though it is usually a good idea to put a time limit on it. But if the discussion is going well as the time limit approaches, you might want to mention it and ask if the group would like to continue the temperature check or move on.

World Heroes

Here is an activity that gets students to think about what it means to be a hero; this version is designed to make sure that they consider heroism and leadership in a global context.

Have students nominate and rank-order 12 males and females as "world heroes." These should be women and men whom the students see as important models for humanity. Encourage students to select people whose lives and accomplishments would be useful to study in a school curriculum designed to help people achieve a sense of community with the whole human race.

Then have students collect for each person nominated: her/his birth date, historical period, a sentence or two of biography, and the students' reasons for nominating that person.

Compare nominations in a classroom discussion. Check to see what time periods, parts of the world, racial groups, and genders are represented most and least. Ask the students what groups would need larger representation in order to have a full picture of global society. Students may also want to speculate about the strengths and weaknesses of their own choices and what those choices reveal to them about the way they see the world.

As a follow-up, discuss the possibility that they themselves might become heroes. How could it happen? Does it seem likely? Would they like to be heroes? What kind of a hero?

In 1985 Tina Turner broke into the Top 20 with the song "We Don't Need Another Hero." Have the students listen to that song and discuss whether they agree or disagree with it. Ask such questions as: Is this a generation that doesn't have or need heroes? Is hero worship dangerous or helpful? What is the function of a hero?

> **Note:** In the PBS series *The Power of Myth* (6 one-hour programs) and in the book of the same name, Joseph Campbell has some wise and interesting things to say about heroes and heroism (see Flowers, Betty Sue, in Resources section). The book chapter (and TV program) that is most directly relevant to heroism is called "The Hero's Adventure." Here Campbell discusses, among other things, why it is necessary to have heroes, what constitutes heroism, and how we can all be heroes.

UNDERSTANDING WORLD ISSUES AND TRENDS

Facts, of and by themselves, are not terribly meaningful. But facts can be potent when viewed in the context of important issues or when they reveal underlying structures and trends in global affairs. The activities in this section offer methods and techniques for grappling with world issues, trends, and systems. The interrelationships which are revealed indicate to us something about the patterns of our lives and the consequences of our actions.

By drawing attention to patterns and consequences of behavior, this section is a logical extension of the previous one. Living responsibly with others requires us to be attentive to how our actions affect others and to be prepared to modify our behavior if we find it is harmful.

Some of the activities, such as "How Many Systems at a Street Corner?," "Our Global Possessions," "Car Watching," and "Millions: Find 'Em and Prove It," provide a variety of strategies for helping students understand the notions of system, structure, and social patterns. These activities include group poster drawing, direct observation, categorizing and mapping, studying the origins of our common possessions, and examining the transnational character of major organizations.

The remaining activities, while they continue to examine issues and/or trends, place greater emphasis on coming to grips with the consequences of our behavior. Again, we provide different techniques for investigating and discussing the topic, including simulations, group discussions, analysis of population growth, and brainstorming.

How Many Systems at a Street Corner?

Life at a street corner, especially in a busy city, can be a dizzying and confusing experience. In fact, it can seem almost terrifying if you are used to the calm of a rural village and then suddenly find yourself in Los Angeles or Mexico City or Barcelona or even Des Moines. But have you ever stopped long enough to notice that all the activity isn't random and chaotic? There are patterns present. And if you stayed long enough to observe, you would notice that the patterns repeat themselves. Of course, on some days the patterns are a little different than on other days. But then you would notice that even though Sunday varies from Wednesday, each Sunday is very much alike and each Wednesday is very much alike.

In each of these patterns there are bits and pieces, parts which go together to make a whole, and these parts are interrelated in such a way that an alteration in one affects others. Each system has its own boundary, yet is also connected to other systems. Understanding the concept of systems is one of the most (some say *the* most) essential learnings for students in a global age. Our planet is one ecological system. International business operates through one huge economic system. These worldwide systems shape and impinge upon more local systems, and vice versa.

So what we have on our street corner are systems. On the next page is a photograph of a street corner. Have the students work in twos or threes to identify all the systems they can. Ask them to explain the parts of the system and how the parts depend on each other.

A picture of a farm or of a natural scene can also be used to demonstrate the presence of systems everywhere. Or you can just take the students outside to the nearest street corner.

Follow up your study of a local street corner with a look at a picture of a street corner in another country. What systems can you find in both places? What differing systems do you note? And what evidence is there of both systems interrelating?

It is much easier to help students understand the idea of systems by inviting them to observe smaller systems, and so a street corner provides a great teaching opportunity. At some point though, you may need to move beyond these tangible examples of systems to more abstract systems such as the global economy.

The "Why" Poster

As teachers, we are always interested in what students are learning. The two most common methods of unearthing this information are giving writing assignments or giving tests. These are fine, but they are not the only ways, and not always the best.

Another method is the group poster, which in this case we call the "Why Poster." You will want to pick a subject appropriate to the age of your students, but let's suppose you are studying the Mexican Revolution. You have spent quite a bit of time talking about Porfirio Diaz, the concentration of wealth and land, the early revolts led by Francisco Madero and Emiliano Zapata, the later violence throughout Mexico, the urban labor movement, the constitutional convention in 1917, the consolidation of the revolution by people like Carranza, Calles, and Obregón, and so on. It's getting to be time to wrap it up. But before that, you want some idea about what the students are learning and what they are mislearning. And you want to do this before the test. So, it's time to have them do a poster. Here is how it works.

Randomly assign students to groups of five. Ask each group to spend some time talking about the major causes of the Mexican Revolution. Or you may want to make this a homework assignment. Tell them to list the major causes on a piece of paper and to bring that to school the next day. Tell them they will be working with four other students to make a poster.

After they have put together a list, they are given a large sheet of paper and several colored markers. Each group is then to draw a poster illustrating what it thinks are the major causes and how the causes are related to each other.

When the drawings are finished, each group should select one or two spokespersons to explain the poster to the rest of the class. As the students discuss the posters, it will be possible for you to get them to understand the complexity of the situation, to review what they have learned, and to correct misimpressions. And you can usually do this without directly criticizing the students or their posters by getting the students to see the similarities and differences in each poster, to see what is omitted, what is important, and what is not important.

Rather than a poster which focuses on causes, you might prefer to have one which identifies the major events of the Revolution, or the major obstacles to change, or the major changes which have occurred as a result of the Revolution. So instead of a Why Poster you could have them do an Events Poster or a Consequences Poster. Whether the object of study is the Mexican Revolution, the breakup of the Soviet Union, rain forest destruction, or the development of the global economy, the poster technique is an excellent approach for a challenging, enjoyable, and effective review of the subject matter.

Population and Exponential Growth

The word "exponent" is used in mathematics to refer to a process of repeated multiplication. For instance, in 10^6, 6 is the exponent and it means that you multiply 10 by itself 6 times: $10 \times 10 \times 10 \times 10 \times 10 \times 10$. Growth in world trade, population growth, increases in energy consumption, and interest compounded in a savings account are examples of exponential growth.

One of the most common examples of exponential growth is in the world's population. For more than two centuries, the exponential rate of population expansion has been written about in dire terms. While many have challenged this pessimistic view, when we look at population growth and, especially, at the "doubling times" for the world's population, it is hard not to be concerned.

Population growth is spoken of as exponential because every year the population is multiplied by the growth rate—the exponent. One simple activity to start talking about exponential growth would be to give the students the current figure for the world's population (5.4 billion) and the current rate of growth, which is 1.7 percent (or .017) per year. Ask them how long it would take, if the growth rate stayed the same, for the world's population to double. If students need help getting started, give them the chart.

> **Note:** Of course, growth rates themselves change, so we have to be careful about making too many predictions based on current growth rates. The tendency has been for the growth rate to get smaller. Nevertheless, the speed of the decrease in the growth rate is slow, so we still keep adding tens of millions of people each year which, of course, increases the population base that produces the growth irrespective of the rate.

Year	World Population
1991	5,300,000,000
1992	5,300,000,000 x 1.017 = 5,390,100,000
1993	5,390,100,000 x 1.017 = 5,481,731,700
1994	5,481,731,700 x 1.017 = ?
1995	? x 1.017 =
1996	

What the students should notice is that, over time, the population is growing a lot faster than they think. A growth rate of 1.7 percent doesn't seem like much. But it gets compounded, and when it does, the growth in total numbers is huge; it is exponential.

One of your students might create a clever visual to illustrate the point. For instance, take a large piece of paper and place red dots on it. Each dot represents 1 million people. Even with each dot representing a million, you will still need 5,300 dots! Now put in the number of dots representing the world's population in 1999, 2099, 2199, 2299, when it will have doubled at the rate of 1.7 percent a year. It might be a bit more manageable, though a little less dramatic, to have each dot represent 10 million or 100 million. You might use different-colored dots for the different years and create a poster.

A few years ago, the population growth rate was 1.9 percent. At that rate, how many years would it take to double? Let us assume that the rate of growth continues to fall so that in a few years the growth rate is 1.5 percent. How many years would it take for the population to double at that rate?

Let us suppose that the world growth rate fell to 1 percent at the time the world population reached 8 billion. By current growth rates, when would the world's population reach 8 billion? At a 1 percent growth rate, how many people would there be the following year? In 10 years? In 20 years?

Ask the students what other sorts of things they think change—including getting smaller—exponentially (such as growth of gross national product, sales of Coca-Cola, depletion of petroleum in a well, water usage, food consumption). Have them bring in some evidence regarding the actual rate of growth.

Women in the World

Much of what we know about people in the world comes from information which is based either on male behavior and thoughts or is presented in gender-neutral language. Until recently, not much effort was expended on supplying information specifically about women. That is now changing. There are books, articles, and atlases which focus on the status of women. Some of these are listed at the end of this activity. Here is some information about women in the world.

- Current data indicate that women make up more than half the world's population, do two-thirds of the world's work (paid and unpaid), but receive only one-tenth of the world's wages.

- The unpaid labor of women in the household, if given economic value, would add an estimated one-third, or $4,000,000,000,000, to the world's annual economic product.

- Rural women account for more than half of the food produced in the Third World and for as much as 80 percent of the food production in Africa.

- The hourly wages of working women in the manufacturing industry are on average three-fourths those earned by men.

- In general, in the United States, women earn 70 percent of each dollar earned by males.

- In 1950 there were 27 million more boys than girls enrolled in primary and secondary levels of education; currently there are 80 million more boys than girls enrolled.

- Both males and females born in developing countries have a shorter life expectancy than babies born in developed countries; for males the average life span is 10 years shorter, for females it is 15 years shorter.

- Nutritional anemia afflicts half of all women of childbearing age in developing countries, compared with less than 7 percent of women of childbearing age in developed countries.

- In the Third World, two-thirds of the women over the age of 25 (and about one-half the men) have never been to school.

- Ten of the 11 oldest democracies in the world did not grant women the right to vote until the 20th century; the first to establish electoral equality was New Zealand (1893), and the last was Switzerland (1971).

- Women are 50 percent of the voting population in the world but hold only about 10 percent of the seats in national legislatures.

150

Here are some ways you might approach this subject.

Allow students 10 minutes in small groups to list questions the foregoing statements raised in their minds. Discuss at least one question from each group.

Two excellent films to prompt further discussion are *Small Happiness* and *Global Assembly Line.* Check with area universities, libraries, county offices of education, or your other best film sources for those titles or for other films about the role of women around the globe. An excellent source for films (and other materials) concerning women is the Women's History Center (see Resources section).

Using either the statistics or a short film as an introduction, ask the students the following questions: Which gender would they choose if they could pick and why? Which gender would they choose if they lived in the Third World and why? When do either women or men encounter injustice as a result of their gender? How does injustice toward one gender serve or hurt the other? Ask them to imagine they are the opposite gender and answer the questions above.

Paul Mayes, an instructor at a local community college, once invited Jan to do a session in his global studies course which was composed equally of men and women. She used this activity. At the end of the semester he called to tell her that half the class (the women) had listed her session as their favorite. "The men," he said, "were pretty well divided between two other sessions."

Some Sources of Information about Women in the World

Bernard, Jessie. *The Female World from a Global Perspective.* Bloomington: Indiana University Press, 1987.

Bourguignon, Erika (Ed.). *A World of Women.* New York: Praeger, 1980.

Charlton, Sue Ellen. *Women in Third World Development.* Boulder: Westview Press, 1984.

Farley, Jennie (Ed.). *Women Workers in Fifteen Countries.* Ithaca, NY: ILR Press, 1985.

Joekes, Susan. *Women in the World Economy—An INSTRAW Study.* New York: Oxford University Press, 1987.

Momsen, Janet. *Women and Development in the Third World.* New York: Routledge, 1991.

Nash, June, and M. Patricia Fernandez-Kelley. *Women, Men and the International Division of Labor.* Albany, NY: SUNY Press, 1983.

Reese, Lyn and Jean Wilkinson. *Women in the World: Annotated History Resources for the Secondary Student.* Metuchen, NJ: Scarecrow Press, 1987.

Sivard, Ruth Leger. *Women...A World Survey.* Washington, DC: World Priorities, 1985.

Women in World Culture Series. Saint Louis Park, MN: Glenhurst Publications.

Women in the World: 1975-1985 and Beyond. Washington, DC: Population Reference Bureau, 1986.

The World's Women: Trends and Statistics, 1970-1990. New York: United Nations, 1991.

151

Firsts

In 1947, Steve's brother was born. In 1950, Steve's family got its first television set. Steve's first trip outside the United States occurred in 1966, and his first child was born in 1969. He first visited Taos, New Mexico, in 1984.

Each of these was a major event for Steve. Each heralded a change in the structure of life that led to doing things and seeing things quite differently from before. Not all firsts are quite so significant, but many are.

And so it is with societies, including nations. Firsts often signal the advent of great changes which will leave the people, their institutions, and their practices substantially altered. Thus, the study of firsts can be an interesting way to study change. Studying firsts can also be an interesting way to understand the historical context of change.

Here are some firsts.

- Hernando Cortés first set foot in Mexico in 1519.

- The first gasoline automobile was built in 1889.

- Women were first given the constitutional right to vote in the United States in 1920.

- In 1945, the United States dropped the world's first wartime atomic bomb.

- The United Nations first officially met in 1945.

- In 1985, for the first time since its early history, the United States became a debtor nation.

- In 1988, for the first time since 1929, the candidate of the dominant party of Mexico officially received less than 60 percent of the vote in the presidential election.

- In 1989, for the first time in 70 years, the Soviet Union conducted contested elections nationwide.

- In 1989, the Soviet Union opened its first Western-style business school.

- In 1990, Beijing opened its first American-style pizza restaurant.

Here are some ways to use this list. Divide the class into several small groups and give each group one of the firsts on this list. Have each group meet and discuss the importance of the first. Following the small-group discussions, have a general class discussion focusing on identifying the keys to what makes a first important. Each group might then do some follow-up research to find the story behind the first and thus place it in its historical context. Or they could gather some information—if it is available—about the consequences of the first.

Here is another idea. Using this list, or one of your own construction as a model, ask the students to identify the 5 or 10 most important firsts during particular periods in world history, in U.S. history, or in the history of other nations. They should be able to explain why they made their selections.

154

The Future Is Transnational?

This activity offers another way to approach and analyze global linkages and to get students thinking about the degree to which the world is moving toward transcending the nation-state and creating truly transnational structures.

Below is a list of acronyms and the full name for each.

ADB	African Development Bank
AI	Amnesty International
ASEAN	Association of Southeast Asian Nations
BIS	Bank of International Settlements
ECDC	Economic Cooperation among Developing Countries
EEC	European Economic Community
G-5	Group of Five
GATT	General Agreement on Tariffs and Trade
GM	General Motors
HPI	Heifer Project International
IDB	InterAmerican Development Bank
IBRD	International Bank of Reconstruction and Development (World Bank)
ICC	International Chamber of Commerce
ICFTU	International Confederation of Free Trade Unions
IMF	International Monetary Fund
ITT	International Telephone and Telegraph
NATO	North Atlantic Treaty Organization
NIEO	New International Economic Order
OECD	Organization for Economic Cooperation and Development
OPEC	Organization of Petroleum Exporting Countries
SALT	Strategic Arms Limitation Talks
SDRs	Special Drawing Rights
SEATO	Southeast Asia Treaty Organization
UNCTAD	United Nations Conference on Trade and Development
UNESCO	United Nations Educational, Scientific and Cultural Organization

WCC	World Council of Churches
WFC	World Food Council
WHO	World Health Organization
YWCA	Young Women's Christian Association

There is much to explore in this list. You might want to give the students just the list of acronyms and see if they can identify them. Then ask them to share anything they know about the purposes of each organization. If this is a list of international and transnational organizations, what is General Motors or ITT doing on the list? Aren't these U.S. corporations? What sorts of changes do these suggest about how the world is structured? And about the meaning of the word "national"? And what about an organization like the EEC? Is this just a collection of nations or is it beginning to assume a life of its own?

While all of these organizations are international in one way or another, they vary substantially in terms of the locus of power. In some cases, the locus is the government of a nation. In other cases, it is a private corporation with power centered in the corporation's headquarters located in one country. In yet other cases, the locus of power is with the headquarters of a private, nonprofit organization. But in some cases, we see evidence of real change as the locus of power moves from a country-based government or home office to a government or home office that is truly transnational (such as the newly created structures of the European Community like the European Development Bank, or global coalition organizations such as Friends of the Earth International). In that sense, which of these organizations are moving to become more transnational? What does it really mean to be transnational? Is the future transnational? Do we want the future to be transnational? Students should discuss these questions in a brainstorming mode first, and then do research projects. For instance, they might explore why the organization came into existence, who was behind it, and what it actually accomplished. Or they might focus on how the organization affects their lives.

156

Gains and Losses

The world is a place of constant change. We can travel around the world faster than ever before and to more places. More and more people are being added to the world's population (there are also more and more places which are looking more and more like each other). We build more skyscrapers and factories and houses and roads and lose more and more farmland and wilderness.

This activity is a variation on the More or Less activity and another good way to start talking about the state of the world and perspective consciousness. It is also a good way to talk about change.

Give the students the list on the following page, adding to it or subtracting from it as you feel appropriate.

Ask the students, in groups of three, to identify those changes which they believe represent true gains (improvements) and those which they think are losses. Have them put all their improvements in one column, all their losses in another. Discuss the results. Why is a change an improvement? A loss? Is there a pattern to their responses?

Next, ask students to compile their own lists of gains and losses. Where will they go to find the information? They can draw examples from their own knowledge and experience, or they can use sources such as almanacs or the *World Eagle* (see Resources section). Then take all their separate lists and combine them into one single list. You may discover some significant differences of opinion.

The items in the large list can be arranged by categories; for instance, those things having to do with transportation, those things having to do with war and peace, those things having to do with the environment, and so on. Experts from the local college or university, from business, from government, or from nonprofit organizations can be invited to give their opinions as to which of these things are really gains and which losses.

Gains and Losses

- The world's population grows by about 1 million persons every 4 days.

- The number of nations in the world has increased from 68 in the 1930s to 191 in 1994.

- In 1990, 41 percent of the people of the world lived in cities; in 1992, 43 percent lived in cities.

- In 1988, the average infant mortality rate for the developing nations was 86 (per 1000 live births). In 1992 the average rate was 75.

- Between 1970 and 1990, worldwide chemical fertilizer usage tripled.

- Each year the amount of land that is desert increases by about 15 million acres.

- To provide the energy for more industry, more jobs, and a better material life, China has greatly increased its use of coal.

- It is estimated that tropical forests once covered 16 percent of the earth's land surface; by 1990 they covered 7 percent of the land surface.

- Japanese direct investment in the United States doubled between 1981 and 1985, to a level of $16 billion.

- In Japan, per capita consumption of steel increased 25 times between 1950 and 1990.

- Over the past 100 years, the global sea level has risen 10-20 centimeters.

- The 1970 average foreign exchange rate for the Japanese yen was 358 to the dollar; by 1990 that had dropped to 145 to the dollar.

- Between 1987 and 1990, the use of marijuana and hashish by U.S. high school students dropped by 20 percent.

- Life expectancy in the less-developed countries has increased by 16 years between 1960 and 1990.

- In the 1980s, the utility industry in the United States used 50 percent less energy than in the previous decade; the chemical industry increased its output by 40 percent and used 26 percent less energy.

Links to the World

How aware are your students of the various ways that the nations and peoples of the world are linked together? Here is a good way to find out. Through five simple and straightforward questions, students in small groups brainstorm all the links they can think of. Because the activity uses small groups and readily lends itself to role assignments within the groups, it is a valuable cooperative learning exercise. For younger groups, it will be necessary to have a discussion about the meaning of the word "impact."

Here is how it works. On 4 x 6 or 5 x 8 cards, write the following instructions, *one instruction per card.*

1. Name some things you do regularly—or that other Americans do—which have an impact on people outside the United States.

   Action   Impact

2. Name some events which occurred outside the United States which have had an impact on your life or the lives of other Americans.

   Event   Impact

3. What articles of clothing or other items do the members of the group have with them that were manufactured outside the United States?

   Item   Country of Manufacture

4. What are the ways that people from different cultures and nations come into contact with one another?

5. What are the common sources of information used by people in the United States to find out what is happening in the world? List these in order from most to least *commonly used.*

Begin by telling the class that you are going to be engaging in an activity called Links to the World. The class will be divided into five smaller groups with each group receiving one question. You are going to read all five questions now to give them a sense of the purpose of the activity. Following this introductory statement, randomly divide the class, hand each group one card, a couple of marking pens, and a piece of newsprint or flip-chart paper.

Tell each group to select a recorder, one or two spokespersons, and people for any other roles (such as timer) you want. Each group brainstorms responses to its question and writes them on the sheet of paper. When the groups are finished, or after some appropriate amount of time, ask the recorder to tape the paper to a wall. Have the spokespersons quickly go over the group's response.

What you do next depends on your interests. Discussing what the students have produced may be sufficient if you simply want them to briefly document global interdependence. Alternatively, each sheet of paper can be viewed as a list of possible research projects. Students' responses to the first item, for instance, suggest a number of ways to study how their behavior affects other parts of the world.

Another sort of research project would be to take one of the questions and use it as the basis of a comparative study. For instance, question 5 asks students to list what they think are the most common sources of information used by people in the United States to find out what is happening in the world. They can ask students from other countries what sources they would list for their countries. If your school does not have many foreign students, consider using international students at the local university or community college.

Question 2 presents a wonderful opportunity for an intergenerational study. Students will be interested in comparing their list of important events with one constructed by their parents or grandparents or by the teachers.

This is a modified version of an activity originally developed by our friends Bob Freeman and Rudie Tretten.

Our Global Possessions

This is another way to document global links. On the wall, place a large map of the world, preferably some interesting projection such as the Peter's Projection. Mention as you begin that the map itself offers a new way of seeing the world and encourage students to examine the map carefully. Then ask each student to select one of his or her possessions and write the item on a piece of Post-it™ paper and then place it on the wall map in the country of origin. Each student should tell the class what his or her item is and where it comes from. This step can be repeated several times if your class is not too large. Then ask students to draw conclusions from the distribution of the sheets of paper.

> Are all regions and countries of the world equally represented? Why not?

> Do certain countries, or regions, seem to be producing certain kinds of goods for the world market? Why would this be true?

> Are items identified in this exercise representative of the exports of the countries?

> Some countries won't be mentioned at all. Does this mean they don't export? How can we find out?

Once this activity is completed, you can use it to introduce a historical comparison. For instance, if we were doing this exercise 10 years ago, would we have the same results? Each student, or each team of 2 or 3 students, could research the exports of certain countries and find out what they exported 10 years ago. A letter to the consulate or embassy of the country might be a good place to start. A visit from a professor of international economics or international business at the local college or university might also make a good beginning.

If you are teaching world history, this activity is an introduction to the concepts of international trade and world marketing. Having some idea of the pattern of international trade today, you might ask what sort of international trade was there in the year 500, in the year 1000, in 1500. And, perhaps, what will it be like in the year 2500?

Mapping the Data

Translating information from statistical tables to a map makes the data available in visual form, helps the students understand it better, and familiarizes them with the nations of the world. This is an activity which can be done with students in a wide range of grade levels and with a myriad of topics.

We have provided data, beginning on page 166, on the infant mortality rate (IMR) for most countries of the world. We have also provided a blank map on page 165. Here is one way to use this information.

First, you want to discuss the term "infant mortality rate." Tell the students that the number refers to the number of infants, one-year-old or younger, who died for each 1000 live births. For instance, the infant mortality rate for Egypt is 73. That means that for every 1000 births in Egypt, 73 infants (one-year-old or younger) die.

Following the discussion, provide each student with a map and then have them map the data on infant mortality rates. Students will need to develop a color code for the different rates so the data can be mapped. For instance, all those nations with an IMR of 10 or fewer could be black; those between 11 and 30, brown; 31-55, blue; 56-80, green; 81-100, red; 101-120, orange; over 120, yellow. (It is helpful if the color coding is set up so that it either goes from darker to lighter or lighter to darker. This permits quicker and easier interpretation.) A word of caution about this sort of exercise. Unless students have clearly seen the significance of the data they're mapping, it could appear to be just so much busywork.

When the students have completed the mapping, ask what conclusions they have reached about infant mortality rates. What guesses, hypotheses, would they make about other aspects of a nation and its IMR? Is there a relationship between GNP per capita and IMR, or between urbanization and IMR? (These can be additional mapping activities.) And so on. Also, be sure to ask whether or not they feel that lumping together countries in a 25-point range is a helpful thing to do. You might note, for instance, that earlier they talked about the difference between the European and U.S. IMRs. But by their color-coded map, there is no difference. Is this a problem? For instance, does it lead us to a simplistic view of the world by minimizing differences?

Of course, some of these questions may not be relevant to your students, but even without a terribly sophisticated discussion, the mapping exercise is useful.

The infant mortality figures on the following pages are from the *World Population Data Sheet* of the Population Reference Bureau, 1992. Other kinds of data to use with this activity can be found in the *World Population Data Sheet,* Ruth Sivard's *World Military and Social Expenditures,* and the various atlases and almanacs cited in the Resources section.

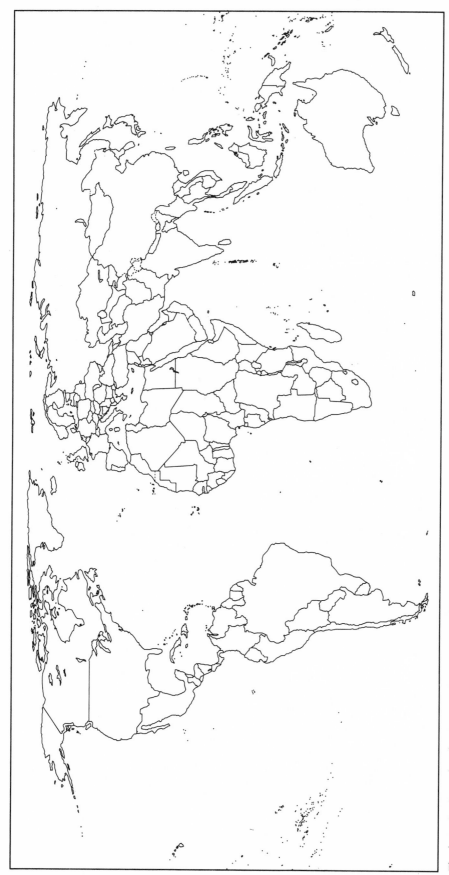

Mapping Data—IMR Chart

AFRICA

Country	IMR	Country	IMR
Algeria	61	Madagascar	115
Angola	132	Malawi	137
Benin	88	Mauritania	122
Botswana	45	Mauritius	20.4
Burkina Faso	121	Morocco	73
Burundi	111	Mozambique	136
Cameroon	85	Namibia	102
Central African Rep.	141	Niger	124
Chad	127	Nigeria	114
Congo	114	Rwanda	117
Côte d'Ivoire	92	Senegal	84
Djibouti	117	Seychelles	13
Egypt	73	Sierra Leone	147
Ethiopia	139	Somalia	127
Equatorial Guinea	112	South Africa	52
Gabon	99	Sudan	87
Gambia	138	Swaziland	101
Ghana	86	Tanzania	105
Guinea	148	Togo	99
Guinea-Bissau	151	Tunisia	44
Kenya	62	Uganda	96
Lesotho	95	Zaire	83
Liberia	144	Zambia	76
Libya	64	Zimbabwe	61

ASIA

Country	IMR	Country	IMR
Afghanistan	172	Mongolia	53
Bangladesh	120	Myanmar	72
Bhutan	142	Nepal	112
Brunei	9	North Korea	31
Cambodia	127	Pakistan	109
China	34	Philippines	54
Hong Kong	6.7	Singapore	6.7
India	91	South Korea	15
Indonesia	70	Sri Lanka	19.4
Japan	4.6	Taiwan	6.2
Laos	112	Thailand	39
Malaysia	29	Vietnam	45
Maldives	34		

EUROPE

Country	IMR	Country	IMR
Albania	30.8	Latvia	19
Austria	7.4	Lithuania	18
Bosnia & Hercegovina	15.2	Luxembourg	7.4
Belgium	7.9	Macedonia	35.3
Bulgaria	14.8	Netherlands	6.8
Croatia	10	Norway	6.9
Czech Republic	11.3	Poland	15.9
Denmark	7.5	Portugal	11
Estonia	25	Romania	25.7
Finland	5.8	Slovakia	11.3
France	7.3	Slovenia	8.9
Germany	7.5	Spain	7.6
Greece	10	Sweden	6
Hungary	15.4	Switzerland	6.8
Iceland	5.9	United Kingdom	7.9
Ireland	8	Yugoslavia (former)	24.4
Italy	8.6		

LATIN AMERICA

Country	IMR	Country	IMR
Argentina	25.7	Guatemala	61
Bahamas	26.3	Guyana	52
Barbados	9	Haiti	106
Belize	32	Honduras	69
Bolivia	89	Jamaica	17
Brazil	69	Mexico	47
Chile	17.1	Nicaragua	61
Colombia	37	Panama	21
Costa Rica	15.3	Peru	76
Cuba	11.1	Puerto Rico	14.3
Dominican Republic	61	Suriname	31
Ecuador	57	Trinidad and Tobago	10.2
El Salvador	55	Uruguay	20.4
Grenada	15.9	Venezuela	24.2
Guadeloupe	9.9		

MIDDLE EAST

Country	IMR	Country	IMR
Bahrain	20	Oman	44
Iran	43	Qatar	26
Iraq	67	Saudi Arabia	65
Israel	8.7	Syria	48
Jordan	39	Turkey	59
Kuwait	16	United Arab Emirates	25
Lebanon	46	Yemen	124

NORTH AMERICA

Country	IMR
Canada	7.1
United States	9

OCEANIA

Country	IMR	Country	IMR
Australia	8	Papua New Guinea	99
Fiji	20	Solomon Islands	32
New Caledonia	18	Vanuatu	32
New Zealand	7.6	Western Samoa	43

FORMER USSR

Country	IMR	Country	IMR
Armenia	35	Moldova	35
Azerbaijan	45	Russia	30
Belarus	20	Tajikistan	73
Georgia	33	Turkmenistan	93
Kazakhstan	44	Ukraine	22
Kyrgyzstan	35	Uzbekistan	64

168

Source: *World Population Data Sheet*. Washington, DC: Population Reference Bureau, 1992.

Mapping the Terminology

Terms like "North," "South," "East," "West," and "Third World" are, or have been, frequently used in the newspapers and magazines, and on radio and television news reports. Although we have some problems with this terminology—or, more precisely, with using these sorts of terms to categorize nations and peoples simplistically—the fact is that a good deal of what is written and said about the world will make very little sense unless one knows to what these terms refer.

There are several ways to go about introducing this language to your students. Here is a multiple-step method. You may wish to use only one or two of these steps.

Begin by asking them if they have ever heard of these terms. If some say they have, then ask what they think their meanings are. If they understand that these terms are used to categorize nations, then ask if they know which nations are "North" (the industrial nations of North America, Europe, and Japan, but sometimes Israel and South Africa are considered "North," as are Australia and New Zealand); which are "South" (mostly the nations of Africa, Asia, Latin America and the Middle East); which nations are "West" (capitalist, also usually democratic, especially Western Europe and North America); and which "East" (formerly the socialist bloc nations of Eastern Europe and the Soviet Union); which belong to the First World (the capitalist, industrialized North), which to the Second (the East), which to the Third World (the South).

As a second step, have students bring in newspaper or magazine articles which use one or more of these terms. How is the term being used? Why does the author use it? Does the term seem to have any particular emotional connotation?

As a third step, give each student a blank map and have the students, with colors or different hash marks or a combination, code the countries. After they have finished, discuss with the students whether they think this terminology and these categorizations are helpful or not. Are there any drawbacks to the categories? When we speak of East vs. West, why does "East" refer to Eastern Europe but not the Middle East or East Asia? Why does "West" not refer to Cuba? Does this make any sense? Do these sorts of divisions lock us into a way of looking at the world that inevitably contributes to a "we vs. they" mentality?

Given the momentous changes in the world since these terms became popular, as a fourth step have the students consider the implications of these changes for this terminology, for the categorization of nations, and even for the alignment of nations. For instance, with the dissolution of the Soviet Union and the revolutionary changes in Eastern Europe, do the terms "East" or "Second World" have any meaning? If not, into what category do we place these countries? Would they fit into the First-World category? The Third World? Or, perhaps, a newly defined Second World (indicating a purely intermediate economic status rather than a socialist one).

The terms "South" and "Third World" have also undergone some alterations because of economic changes in parts of Asia, Africa, and Latin America. A few of the countries in these areas have achieved a high enough level of industrialization and economic strength to be referred to as Newly Industrialized Countries (NICs). South Korea, Taiwan, Singapore, and frequently Brazil and Mexico are included in this category. At the other end of the continuum are those countries which have suffered serious economic blows. They are the poorest of the poor and are often referred to as the Fourth World. What are the implications of the fact that some countries have graduated from Third-World to NIC status while others have fallen to Fourth-World status? Are there other changes occurring which suggest the need for other terms? Can we do without these sorts of terms?

This activity will be a good introduction both to the current, prevalent terminology and to the location of the world's countries—and to some fundamental problems in our worldview.

Car Watching

At any age we demonstrate a curiosity about and an interest in the world around us. The ability to collect data and draw conclusions about it is a basic skill that any globally educated student needs. Even seven- and eight-year-olds are researchers of sorts. For example, children do a great deal of socializing in places where they can watch and comment on passing cars. We can use the kind of curiosity expressed in this pastime to help students increase their competence in collecting information about the world, hone their skill at research and measurement, and develop an attitude of inquiry—which will be useful to them throughout their lives—as a means of getting to know the larger world around them.

Here's a fairly detailed format to help students learn from car watching. Ask them if they ever sat on a street corner talking with their friends and noticing or commenting on passing automobiles. Let students relate some of their experiences. Then tell the students that you would like them to do some car watching for a half hour or an hour and report back to class the next day. Have them count something that catches their attention. Below are some examples of what might be counted, but there are many, many more possibilities.

- Number of people in each car.

- Number of cars going in each direction at particular times of the day.

- Number of women drivers.

- Number of men drivers.

- Percentage of cars with children in them. Have one or two count all the cars and one or two others count only those with children in them.

- Percentage of cars that are imports.

- Percentage of cars that are red.

When they bring their data in, it can be recorded on the board or duplicated so that the information is available to all students for analysis.

Ask the students to make some hypotheses about the people in the community using the data they have collected. Some examples are:

- People mostly drive south in the afternoon.

- People in town prefer red cars to any other color.

- More people buy imports than U.S.-made cars.

- Most adults have children.

172

If students have a difficult time generating hypotheses, you might have them pretend to be people from another planet who have made these observations to report back to their planet's leaders. Also ask them to suggest ways to further test the hypotheses. What additional information would be needed to see if the hypotheses are really correct? What other kinds of research activities would they need to carry out?

In concluding the discussion, ask the students if they know what a census is. Do they think the data they gathered is similar in any way to the data collected in a census?

To add an international dimension to this activity, you can provide students with one or more photos of traffic scenes in Tokyo, London, Paris, Mexico City, Nairobi, and so forth and see if they can determine any differences or develop other hypotheses.

Buy a Buck

Here is a simulation to help students understand some of the assumptions and the psychology of an arms race. The cold war is said to be over, but the accumulated weapons still exist and cold-war thinking will affect attempts at arms reduction. Moreover, arms races between nations other than superpowers also occur.

Begin by telling the students that you are going to auction a fresh new dollar bill to the highest bidder. Ask who in the class would be interested in bidding for the dollar. Pick two highly motivated students to play. You can pick more than two, but two usually is enough to demonstrate certain aspects of arms-race decision making. (Note: Be sure that you will not be violating any school regulations or norms by conducting this auction.)

Explain the rules that apply to the auction. You might even post the rules on the board.

1. The bidding will begin with a nickel. Each additional bid may be at any amount, from a penny up.

2. The dollar goes to the highest bidder.

3. The second highest bidder also must pay the auctioneer the amount he or she bid. (This rule is not common in auctions.) Make sure students are very clear about this rule.

Having clearly explained the rules, you are now ready to conduct the auction. If the bidders operate with the assumptions that guide an arms race, they will likely end up bidding more than a dollar for the dollar bill you are offering. That is what you want. If they don't bid more than a dollar, their behavior will still serve as a basis for talking about the assumptions and beliefs that would result in people bidding more than a dollar, and those are the assumptions you are trying to identify. If the bidders end the bidding before either has bid a dollar or more, remind the lower bidder that he or she will lose the money bid. Ask if they would like to go higher.

When the bidding has been completed, the money collected, and the dollar given to the higher bidder, hold a discussion about the game. Here are some questions you might want to ask:

- What does someone have to be thinking to spend more than one dollar to get a dollar?

- Consider the arms race between the United States and the former Soviet Union; in what ways were the assumptions of the two countries like those of the participants in the auction?

- If no one would spend more than a dollar to get the dollar, why?

174

- What assumptions and beliefs would have to change in order to stop an arms race?

- Can an arms race be stopped or only slowed down?

- Would slowing down an arms race release resources for social needs?

When the discussion has been completed or at the end of the class period, return all the money, stating that you were only playing a game.

Forecasts for the Year 2030

Often activities which utilize future scenarios are so fanciful that it is difficult to see what learning value is involved. The format of this exercise offers a way to engage students in thinking about the future in the context of current conditions and recent trends and in examining their attitudes toward changes that are taking place. It will also aid them in clarifying their values and in developing a sense of what the future outcomes of these conditions or trends are likely to be.

Each statement below describes a possible condition in the year 2030. For each statement, mark in the left-hand column with an X or a check whether you approve or disapprove. Make the mark even if it seems obvious what the response should be. In the right-hand column mark whether you think the condition will or will not exist.

Approve	Disapprove		Will exist	Will not exist
_____	_____	1. The present world population of 5.4 billion will have increased by at least 50 percent, and will be at least 11 billion.	_____	_____
_____	_____	2. The present U.S. population of 248 million will have increased more slowly than the world as a whole and will be about 330 million.	_____	_____
_____	_____	3. Population will have grown faster than the ability to produce food and in some parts of the world millions will be dying of hunger.	_____	_____

Approve	Disapprove		Will exist	Will not exist
_____	_____	4. American per capita income will have doubled from $22,000 to $44,000 (in constant dollars).	_____	_____
_____	_____	5. Per capita income in the developing nations will have doubled, from $810 to $1620.	_____	_____
_____	_____	6. A few of the Third-World nations will be wealthier and more industrialized; many will be poorer.	_____	_____
_____	_____	7. Air and water pollution will be much worse because nations industrializing and updating agriculture cannot afford pollution controls.	_____	_____
_____	_____	8. Global reserves of many important nonrenewable natural resources such as oil, natural gas, aluminum, lead, and tin will be exhausted.	_____	_____
_____	_____	9. There will have been several serious accidents at nuclear power stations involving radioactive contamination of the surrounding areas.	_____	_____
_____	_____	10. Almost all nations will possess nuclear weapons.	_____	_____
_____	_____	11. Values will have changed so that Americans no longer judge their personal worth in terms of material possessions and financial success.	_____	_____
_____	_____	12. Europeans will think of themselves as Europeans and not as Germans or Britons, etc.	_____	_____

Approve   Disapprove   Will exist   Will not exist

_____ _____ 13. Most pollution, food, and   _____ _____
energy problems will
have been solved by sci-
entific and technological
breakthroughs.

_____ _____ 14. People will be as con-   _____ _____   **177**
cerned about the welfare
of those in other parts of
the world as they are
about the welfare of their
fellow citizens.

After the students have completed marking their responses, place
them in groups of about five and ask them to discuss their responses. Each group should select someone to record the number
of responses in each column. After the groups have had adequate
time to allow each person an opportunity to discuss his or her
responses to at least a few of the items and after a complete tally
has been completed, return to the full group. Here are some suggestions for discussion topics in the full group:

- Which items generated the most consensus? Why?

- Which items generated the least consensus? Why?

- Which of the conditions do you think most likely to occur?
  Which least likely? Why?

- What kinds of information do we need to help us determine
  the probability of any of these occurring? For instance, for
  numbers 1 and 2, what kinds of information do we need?
  What kinds of information do we need for 13 and 14?

- Of those conditions most likely to occur, which concern you
  the most?

Millions: Find 'Em and Prove It

Everywhere you look these days you see reference to millions of this and billions of that. According to a report issued by Policy Analysis for California Education, California has 1.78 million children living in poverty. Recent demographic studies estimate that the population of Mexico City is 20 to 22 million. It is widely reported that 65 percent of all Brazilians, about 100 million people, are malnourished. According to the 1992 *World Almanac*, there are 1.6 million hospital beds in Japan and 1.3 million hospital beds in the United States, which, by the way, has twice the population of Japan. There were 134 million telephones in the United States, but for the more than 1 billion Chinese, there were only 2.4 million telephones. A few years ago Peter Drucker, a well-known authority on business management, estimated that world trade in currencies was of the order of $80 to $100 trillion per year.

Some of the information above is fascinating; some of it is quite disturbing. And these kinds of facts and figures bombard us constantly. But how real are they? Can you imagine actually going around Brazil, every inch of the Amazon, counting all the people who are malnourished? If you have ever been to Mexico City, with the population so widely spread out and with multiple families living in dwellings hidden among shops and back alleys, you would see how absurd it is to ever know the actual population of the place. It is certainly very big, and an estimate such as 20 million has some meaning. But it could just as easily be 18 million or 24 million.

In an article in *Time* magazine a few years ago, Otto Friedrich made the following argument about the precision of much of the information we encounter:

> In almost any area of life today, the best—certainly the most honest—answer to a request for figures would be: Nobody knows. But that makes us feel that somebody has failed at his job; there must be a right answer, therefore a right answer is composed. Last week the Federal Government's Center for Disease Control announced that a certain drug company may have infected 5,000 hospital patients with contaminated intravenous solutions, contributing to the

deaths of 500 people. When asked how this figure had been determined, a Government spokesman said that one estimate of 2,000 was unrealistic and another estimate of 8,000 was unfair. So the authorities split the difference.

A slightly aged joke conveys a similar point. Someone asked a TV weatherperson how she was able to determine that there was an 80 percent chance of rain as had just been predicted. The reply was that there were 10 people working at the station and 8 of them thought it was going to rain!

A very important facet of critical thinking is for students to come to understand the limits of data collection. Numbers should not necessarily be rejected out of hand. But they should always be questioned. Here is one way to go about doing so.

Begin by having students bring into class an article that talks about a million or billion of something or at least an article which relies heavily on numerical information. What is known about how the researchers collected the information? Do the students think it is accurate? Why or why not? Is some information likely to be more accurate than other information? What conditions are conducive to accuracy? To distortions?

Following this initial discussion, divide the students into groups of twos or threes and ask each group to go outside, find a million of something, and prove it. It could be a million blades of grass in a student's front yard or the city park; it could be a million grains of sand; a million Hershey bars in the local grocery stores. Before the exercise, you might want to talk about sampling; students should know that in most studies, the researchers attempt to count people or hospital beds or whatever in some small sample and then make a general estimate based on the sample results. You can also send them out first and then talk about sampling after they return.

When the students have completed their counting, allow ample time to discuss the experience. What kinds of things did students attempt to count? Did they begin to count one item and then switch to another? Why? How many students feel they accurately counted a million of their item? If there are persons who feel they were accurate, ask how they know. What process did they use for proof? What are the implications of this exercise for assessing the meaning or reliability of data they are bombarded with about world issues?

News from the Past

When we were kids, Edward R. Murrow and then Walter Cronkite hosted a TV program called *You Are There.* Each episode focused on a major historical event (the defeat of the Spanish Armada, the battle of Concord and Lexington) as if it were being reported by a team of modern TV newscasters. It was wonderful, being taken back in time to view important events of the past through a modern lens.

More recently, PBS has developed several video programs called *Newscasts from the Past.* These, like the earlier CBS program, fall into the category of "docudrama"; that is, they are designed as if news reporters were around in ancient times interviewing participants in important events such as the Aztec conquest of the Toltecs, Thomas à Becket's flight to France, the Children's Crusade, the first death from the Black Plague, the Spanish Inquisition, and so on. The six 15-minute videos cover the period from 1148 to 1650. The videos are truly global in that each depicts contemporaneous events in different parts of the world.

This is a marvelous format for making history come alive. Obtain one or more of the videos to show as a model. Then break the students into groups of five or six and assign each group, or have each group choose, an important international event or a month or year in the past when important international events took place. Have the students research as much as they can about what happened, who did what, who wrote what. Virtually all of this information will, of course, focus on the major actors in the event, and the views will be those of educated and typically powerful, prosperous, and privileged persons. What can students find out about what the average person was doing? How might a peasant farmer have reacted to the news?*

Out of their research, students create their own docudramas. One student in each group should be the reporter while each of

---

Civilization and Capitalism: 15th-18th Century, the three-volume study of the social and material history of the fifteenth to eighteenth centuries by the late French historian, Fernand Braudel, is a valuable source for this kind of information. See Resources section.

the others will play the roles of one or two participants in or observers of the event. When the skits have been completed, discuss the project. How well do they think they were able to portray the point of view of the person they were representing? Are there feelings or ideas they couldn't recreate because of the time that has elapsed or because of differences in culture and/or perspective between the students and people of the period in which the event occurred? What frustrations did they experience in gathering information? What sorts of things do we know well about the past? What sorts of things do we not know very well, or at all? When we become history, will the gaps in knowledge be the same or will the future know more about us than we know about our past? Why?

182

EXPANDING THE CAPACITY TO CHANGE

There is no learning without change. In fact, change is inherent in the learning experience, and the more comfortable one is with change the easier it is to learn. Much adult resistance to learning, compared to the phenomenal rates of early childhood learning, has to do with the resistance to or fear of change. Because change is so fundamental to the learning process, all the activities in this book have something to do with it.

What the activities in this section do, at least in part, is to place the learner in an explicit, acknowledged context of change and then invite him or her to confront (gently) that context. This is particularly true of "Do You Have to…to…?," "Personal Time Lines," and "Hero, Victim, Fool."

Besides its connection to learning, confronting change is important because the extent and rate of change in the world today are unprecedented. As noted in the introduction, many experts claim that people today have to adapt to changes which come more quickly and in larger numbers than at any previous time in human history. As one examines the sorts of trends included in the activities in the previous section, these notions about change inevitably arise. So the activities in this section simply deal with the phenomenon explicitly and invite the students to think about the future in which they will live.

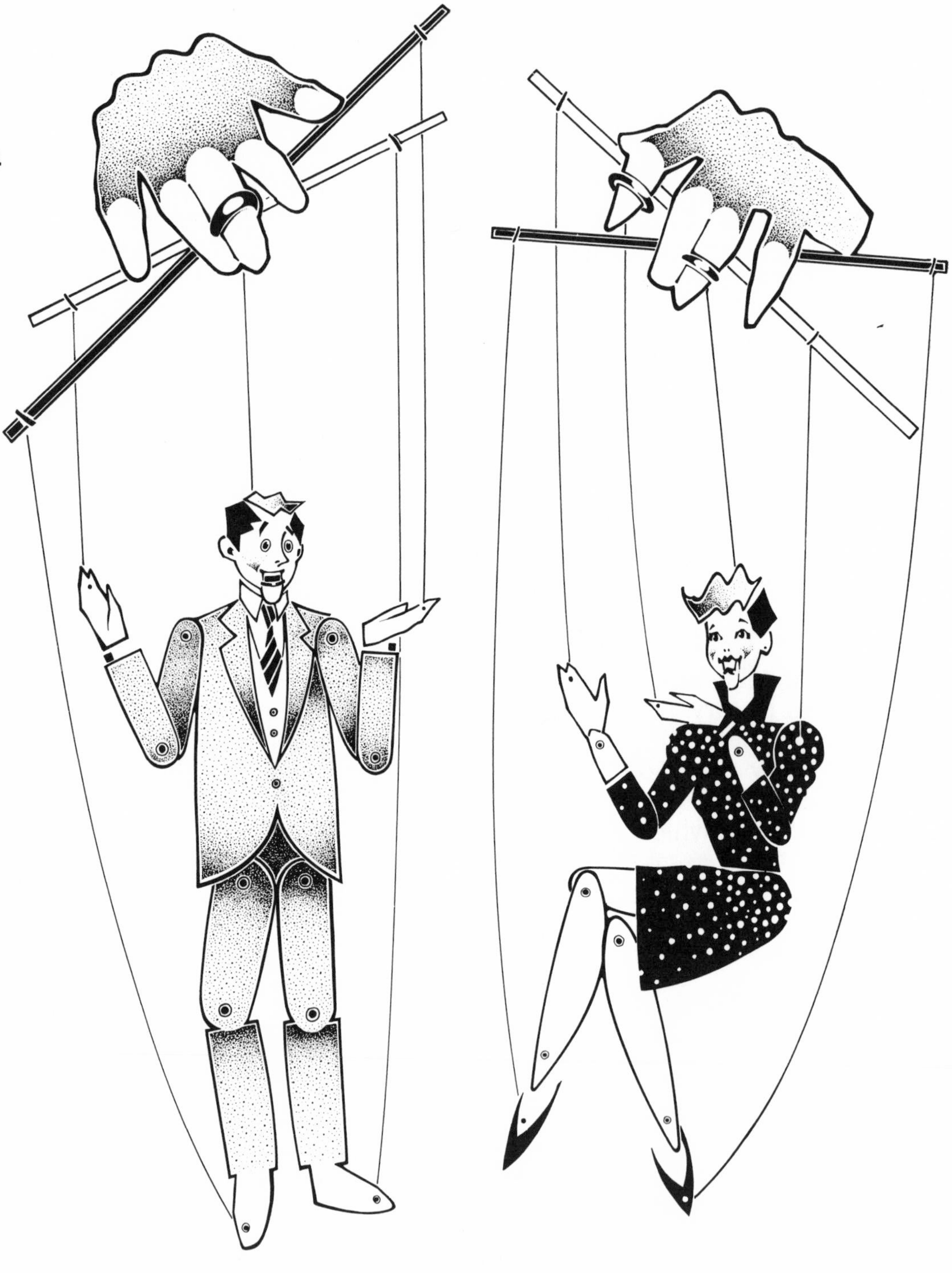

Do You Have to...to...?

Dealing with global issues shows us that mistaken beliefs and carelessly held assumptions often plague modern thought. We believe it is critical, therefore, to explore the intellectual habits and the mental obstacles that keep us from thinking clearly.

This exercise is designed to get students to think about unquestioned assumptions. It is particularly good with elementary students.

A neat technique for challenging assumptions is contained within the simple yet thought-provoking question, "Do you have to...to...?" For example:

1. Do you have to go to school to be smart?

2. Do you have to give the right answer to be right?

3. Do you have to be a girl to play with dolls?

4. Do you have to be sad to cry?

5. Do you have to be a Christian to believe in God?

6. Do you have to work hard to get rich?

7. Do you have to be rich to be happy?

8. Do you have to be a man to be President?

9. Do you have to get caught to be a thief?

10. Do you have to go to college to get a good job?

11. Do you have to go to war to settle international disputes?

12. Do you have to be born in America to be an American?

13. Do you have to cut forests to have enough building materials?

We think there are a number of good ways to use this simple technique. Take some of the questions—or make up your own—and poll the class. Then discuss why some people said yes and others no. (Remember, there are no wrong answers here.)

Another idea. Have your class brainstorm their own list of "Do you have to...to..." questions to discuss or just to help them become more aware of how assumptions influence thinking. With older students, you might prefer to have them brainstorm ideas that they hold as true which may not be—ideas that are so commonly held to be true they have become myths, a part of the unconscious mental framework for understanding our lives and the world, for example, peace will result from more international contact and understanding; English will become the world language and solve all our communication problems; most of the world's problems could be solved if more aid were given to developing countries; husband, wife and children constitute a family.

A final suggestion. Younger students probably need to focus only on broadening the possibilities close at hand with their "Do you have to" questions. Older students can begin to explore the larger world, as suggested by questions 11, 12, and 13 and most of the examples in the previous paragraph.

Scarcity Thinking

This is another activity that enables people to explore conventional wisdom and unquestioned assumptions. Here we focus on one pervasive assumption, the assumption of scarcity.

First we tell the students that each of them is the sole ruler of a nation and must allocate percentages of his or her nation's resources to the categories listed, plus any he or she wishes to add. The list of percentages should total 100. They are given only 5 minutes to make the decision. There is, of course, much moaning and groaning, which we counter by pointing out that no ruler ever has enough time to decide.

Government Service Area	Percentage of Budget
• Endowment for the arts (music, painting, dance, theater...)	_____
• Roads and highways	_____
• Military forces	_____
• Medical care and research	_____
• Education	_____
• Endowment for the humanities (literature, philosophy, history...)	_____
• Endowment for the sciences	_____
• Postal system	_____
• Welfare system	_____
• Public transportation	_____

When they have completed their list, they are grouped in threes and told that they are now part of a ruling junta that must negotiate and agree upon the allocations. After another 5 minutes, we stop the discussion to ask 3 questions.

1. How many people, when doing the exercise alone, had to allocate less than they wanted to some categories?

2. How many people had to allocate less than they wanted when they worked in threes?

3. How did they know the percentage(s) in question represented less than enough?

After a bit of struggling with the third question, someone is likely to realize that they had assumed there were scarce resources.

We call this activity "Scarcity Thinking." The assumption of scarce resources pervades much of modern decision making and is used and misused in the service of power. In fact, the notion of scarcity is one of the core concepts of the entire field of economics. Virtually all economic textbooks begin by telling you that there are always more needs than there are resources to meet them.

Of course, there is often a good deal of truth to the assumption of scarcity, especially if we substitute the word "wants" for "needs." But is scarcity always the case? Are there cases (oil, for example, or diamonds) where scarcity has been created? Are there structures which exist which are designed to create scarcity, such as the number of contestants who can win a game or the number of students who can get good grades if the teacher uses a "curve"? Once students identify the idea of scarcity thinking and scarcity structures, they will quickly be able to tell you other places where it prevails. Take time also to identify resources that aren't or don't have to be scarce—beauty, intelligence, fun, love.

> **Note:** There are many people who have consistently challenged scarcity thinking. For instance, see Julian Simon, *The Ultimate Resource,* Princeton: Princeton University Press, 1981.

Personal Time Lines

189

This is an activity that is particularly good for use with older students or educators in exploring the ways we think of history. At the end, we suggest an alternative format for the exercise which works well with younger students.

Since it involves participants introducing themselves, it is a good exercise to use at or near the beginning of a workshop or institute. Classes can use it at the beginning of the term. Here is how it works.

Ask the participants to think about the 7 (or 5 or 10) most important events in their own lives. They might want to ponder this awhile and then list them on a piece of scratch paper; some gentle background music can aid reflection. Next, with a large piece of paper (such as flip-chart or newsprint) and with several colored markers, they are to make a time line illustrating these 7 events.

Some will make a time line which moves straight from left to right or top to bottom. Others might make a wavier line indicating highs and lows in their lives. Some people will make spirals; yet others will make lines that look like an EKG readout.

The different forms provide a perfect way to talk about how we perceive history. Of course, you must provide time for each person to share his or her life with others. After this, talk about the different styles of time lines. Why did people draw them the way they did? What assumptions, conscious or not, went into each person's arrangement of dates and events? Which of the different kinds of time lines most accurately represents historical flow? Do we always go from past to present to future? And do we always do so in a sort of straight line? Is it possible to think of history in cyclical patterns? What about the seasons? Are history and progress essentially the same?

At the high school level, this activity could be followed by introducing students to visions of history developed by some of the world's great historians. Some see history unfolding in a predetermined fashion, with little human impact on its course. Others believe humans have more control over history. And so on. You might give students excerpts from some of the world's great historians to demonstrate different ways of thinking about history. These could include Confucius, Kalhana (India), Thucydides,

Livy, Ibn Khaldun (Tunisia), Edward Gibbon, Karl Marx, Henry Adams, Oswald Spengler, Arnold Toynbee, Barbara Tuchman.

A variation on this activity works quite well with younger children. Have them draw panels of pictures, like a banner, which include important events in their lives and things they look forward to happening or that they expect to happen.

Hero, Victim, Fool

Here is a particularly enjoyable and useful format for learning about your students, for raising notions about heroes and heroines, about myths, and about the ways societies victimize people or that people victimize themselves. It is also quite an intriguing way for raising questions about the process of categorization.

George developed this activity by making slides of well-known figures—athletes, politicians, performers, religious leaders, and so forth—from around the world. The covers of magazines such as *Time, Sports Illustrated,* and *People* are an excellent source. The slides are shown to the students and, following each slide, the students are to say whether, for them, the person is a hero, a victim, or a fool.

As the students give their responses, talk about why they see the person as they do. Usually, there will be disagreement, which allows you the opportunity to probe and get them to see how different perceptions are formed. Also, you can ask them what sorts of myths have developed concerning the individuals and the extent to which they accept the myth. And—how do people become victims? Is there something about the way society functions that makes the person a victim?

Typically, at some point during the discussion, some students will become frustrated by the hero-victim-fool choice. They want to be able to use other terms. It might be useful here to stop and ask why they are getting frustrated. Are there other kinds of categorization that frustrate them? What about grades? What about political labels?

As an alternative to making the slides yourself, or as a follow-up activity, you could have students collect photos and show them, or you could make the slides from their photos.

Do We Mean What We Say?

One of the first tasks facing global educators is to help people figure out what sorts of obstacles keep them from thinking clearly about their world. For instance, one struggle Americans have is a kind of "everybody's nice" predisposition. At worst, that assumption can lead to some very naive bad judgments; at the very least, it can lead people to miss a lot of what is going on around them. Most of our experience is complex and interesting rather than merely nice.

Students need to learn to question, to notice when their experience doesn't confirm the accuracy of what they are being told. They need to learn that quite often the rhetoric of people who speak to the public and of many public figures doesn't match their practice.

In fact, we worry sometimes that people have become so accustomed or numbed to this disparity between what is said and what is meant that it has become almost impossible to think clearly about what is going on in the world.

There are many instances when we wish people would act as if they mean what they say. Perhaps you might explore the following possibilities with your students.

- If the banker really meant it when he said, "We want to do what's good for you," what would happen?

- If the football coach really meant it when he said, "My most important job is to help build the character of these young men," what would happen?

- If world leaders really meant it when they said they want peace, what would happen?

Once you have invited students to be skeptical, bring in a stack of newspapers and invite them to find things they don't believe. Have them work in teams of two or three. For each item they find, they must provide 3 to 5 distinct reasons for their disbelief. They can call on conflicting data, opposing expert testimony, their own contradicting experience, or some of each.

Two caveats accompany this activity. One of its strengths and weaknesses is that students may want to draw on prejudice and stereotypes to justify their opinions. Be ready to question the questioners. A second caution—some people use skepticism as an excuse for indecision and inaction. You may want to conclude by suggesting that students make a final statement about something they do believe and may want to act on.

Finally, one more idea for students who enjoy music. They could find a song that expresses skepticism ("Say What You Mean and Mean What You Say" by The Fixx is one example) and create a slide show to go with the music, or produce an MTV-style video.

Multiple Views

The purposes of this activity are to help students understand the nature and sources of bias and explore multiple perspectives. We have suggested a particular issue to serve as the subject matter for the activity. As you will see, however, the format can be used for any issue.

One of the most difficult human and political issues facing the United States and many other nations is that of immigration. As governments continue to grapple with budget deficits, with increased demands on social services, and with increasing ethnic tensions, the question of whether to limit immigration becomes particularly salient.

This activity requires students to gather legal and statistical information about immigration. In the United States, two legal documents are particularly pertinent. The Immigration Reform and Control Act of 1986, also known as the Simpson-Mazzoli bill, is the controlling piece of legislation governing immigration policy. Students should also obtain or be provided copies of the Convention on the Status of Refugees. This document, adopted by the United Nations in 1951, exemplifies the efforts to articulate the rights of refugees.

Information about immigration issues can be obtained from many other sources. We have listed some at the end of this exercise. In addition, the *Opposing Viewpoints* series by Greenhaven Press (see Resources section) contains a volume entitled *Immigration.*

When students have gathered the information, have them write a response from two perspectives, selecting from the following list (to which you may wish to add):

- a poor person from Haiti seeking refuge in the United States

- an immigrant from Vietnam

- a conservative presidential candidate

- a member of the staff of the American Friends Service Committee

- a farmer who relies heavily on immigrant labor from Mexico

- an officer of the Border Patrol

- an American taxpayer who believes we spend too much money on social services

As an interesting comparison, ask students how their own ideas match the ones expressed in their response.

This format can be adapted with almost endless variation. One is to create additional roles so that each student, or each small group of students, is assigned a particular role. Each "actor" writes a review of the information, and then they all attend a conference to present and debate their points of view. How would the students go about trying to write a consensus report?

Another alternative is to have the students represent different nations at an international conference on refugees. Data about the problem of international refugees can be obtained from the United Nations High Commission on Refugees (154, rue de Lausanne, Case Postale 2500, -1211 Geneva 2, Switzerland) and from several of the organizations cited below. Students should read the Convention on the Status of Refugees and then meet to determine if the Convention should be revised, given recent experiences.

Sources for Data on Immigration and Refugees

American Friends Service Committee (AFSC)
1501 Cherry St.
Philadelphia, PA 19102

American Immigration Control Foundation (AICF)
PO Box 525
Monterey, VA 24465

American Immigration Institute
1625 K St. N.W., Room 380
Washington, DC 20006

Center for U.S.-Mexican Studies
University of California, San Diego
La Jolla, CA 92093

Refugee Policy Group
1424 16th St. N.W., Suite 401
Washington, DC 20002

Refugee Women in Development
810 First St. N.E., Suite 300
Washington, DC 20002

The U.S. Committee for Refugees
1025 Vermont Ave. N.W.
Washington, DC 20005
Publishes the annual *World Refugee Survey.*

Multiple Views and Fairy Tales

In the previous activity we described a role-play method for students to examine sources of bias and to experience multiple viewpoints. An enjoyable variation for exploring multiple viewpoints that works with younger students is to have them tell familiar fairy tales, such as *Cinderella* or *The Three Bears,* from the viewpoint of various characters. For example, Cinderella's story might sound quite different told from the stepmother's point of view.

One way to do this is to assign a particular character in a fairy tale to a small group of students. Let them retell the story from the point of view of that character. Other groups can be assigned different characters.

A variation of this is to have groups depict a *scene* in the fairy tale from a particular character's point of view. These depictions can be drawn on a large sheet of butcher paper. After the drawings have been completed, one or two spokespersons from the group can explain the point of view.

Another variation would be to call a "council of the characters" to have them give their reactions to the events in the story. Students are given time to prepare their viewpoint and then relate their feelings and thoughts about the way the event unfolded.

A good source of international tales is the Wright Group's series "Traditional Tales from around the World." (The Wright Group, 10949 Technology Place, San Diego, CA 92127.) The series includes tales from South Asia, the British Isles, the Mediterranean, and the Caribbean.

Group Poem

Here is a wonderful way to get to know your students and to get information from them about what they learned from a unit or during the semester or during the school year. It is also a very effective way to conclude a workshop, retreat, camp, or institute.

On the blackboard, write the following phrases: I saw..., I heard..., I learned..., I am.... Ask the students to complete each of these phrases with just one or two words. It works best if each student has four separate slips of paper. It is important that you make the reference clear for what it is that they saw, heard, and so forth. Is it in terms of the recently completed field trip? The unit they just completed? The past semester? We sometimes allow a reflective time before the actual writing activity during which we guide their reminiscence of the experience we're asking them to write about.

After the students have completed their writing, take the slips, (or for a shorter version take each person's favorite of the four), arrange them under the four headings and then read them back. With proper emphasis on repetitive words and cadences, you will have a group poem. If you wish, you can take the slips home and arrange them in an order that you find particularly effective. This is also a good way to encourage students to express themselves through poetry.

200

Resources

Theory and Practice of Global Education

Ad Hoc Committee on Global Education. "Global Education: In Bounds or Out." *Social Education* 51 (April/May 1987).

American Council on Education and the Education Commission of the States. *One-Third of a Nation: A Report of the Commission on Minority Participation in Education and American Life.* Washington, DC: American Council on Education, 1988.

Anderson, Charlotte. "Global Education in the Classroom." *Theory into Practice* 21 (Summer 1982).

Banks, James, and Cherry Banks, eds. *Multicultural Education: Issues and Perspectives.* Boston: Allyn and Bacon, 1989.

Bergen, Timothy, Jr. "Education at the International Level." *International Education* 20 (Spring 1991).

Blackburn, Anne. "Expanding Viewpoints: The Global Environment." *Curriculum Review* 25 (November/December 1985).

Carse, James. *Finite and Infinite Games.* New York: The Free Press, 1986.

Cogan, John. "Global Education: Opening Children's Eyes to the World." *Principal* 61 (November 1981).

Costa, Arthur. "Teaching for Intelligence." *In Context* 18 (Winter 1988).

Ehrlich, Paul, and Robert Ornstein. *New World, New Mind.* New York: Doubleday, 1988.

Global Pages. Immaculate Heart College Center, 10951 W. Pico Blvd., Los Angeles, CA 90064. Quarterly.

Hanvey, Robert. "An Attainable Global Perspective." *Theory into Practice* 21 (Summer 1982).

Kniep, Willard. "Global Education in the Eighties." *Curriculum Review* 25 (November/December 1985).

Lamy, Steven. "Defining Global Education." *Educational Research Quarterly* 8 (1983).

Merryfield, Merry. "Preparing Social Studies Teachers for the Twenty-First Century: Perspectives on Program Effectiveness from a Study of Six Exemplary Teacher Education Programs in Global Education." *Theory and Research in Social Education* 1 (Winter 1992).

Orr, David. "What Is Education for?" *In Context* 27 (Fall 1990).

Palmer, Parker. "Good Teaching: A Matter of Living the Mystery." *Change: The Magazine of Higher Learning* (January/February 1990).

Pike, Graham, and David Selby. *Global Teacher, Global Learner.* London: Hodder and Stoughton Educational, 1989.

Rosenau, James. "Teaching and Learning in a Transnational World." *Educational Research Quarterly* 8, no. 1 (1983).

Simonson, Rick, and Scott Walker, eds. *Multi-Cultural Literacy.* St. Paul: Graywolf Press, 1988.

Weiner, G., ed. *Just a Bunch of Girls.* Philadelphia: Open University Press, 1985.

Almanacs, Atlases, and Other Resources

Allen, John. *Student Atlas of World Politics.* Guilford, CT: Dushkin Publishing Group, 1991.

Barnaby, Frank. *The Gaia Peace Atlas.* New York: Doubleday, 1988.

Braudel, Fernand. *Civilization and Capitalism: 15th-18th Century.* New York: Harper and Row, 1984.

Brown, Osa. *Metropolitan Museum of Art Activity Book: Crafts, Models, Toys, Games, Puzzles, and Mazes Inspired by the Treasures in the Museum's Collection.* New York: Random House, 1983.

Church World Service. *Make a World of Difference: Creative Activities for Global Learning.* New York: Friendship Press, 1990.

Crow, Ben, and Alan Thomas. *Third World Atlas.* Philadelphia: Open University Press, 1983.

Culturgrams. David M. Kennedy Center for International Studies, Brigham Young University, Provo, UT 84602.

Elder, Pamela, and Mary Ann Carr. *Worldways: Bringing the World into the Classroom.* Menlo Park, CA: Addison-Wesley, 1987.

Fenton, Thomas, and Mary Heffron. *Latin America and the Caribbean: A Directory of Resources.* New York: Orbis Books, 1986.

Flowers, Betty Sue, ed. *The Power of Myth: Joseph Campbell, with Bill Moyers.* New York: Doubleday, 1988.

Fluegelman, Andrew. *The New Games Book.* Garden City, NY: Doubleday, 1976.

_____ *More New Games! —and Playful Ideas from the New Games Foundation.* Garden City, NY: Doubleday, 1981.

Fowler, Virginia. *Folk Toys around the World and How to Make Them.* Englewood Cliffs, NJ: Prentice-Hall, 1984.

Harper's. 666 Broadway, New York, NY 10012; monthly. See "Harper's Index."

Harper's Index Book, The. New York: Henry Holt, 1987.

Hoffman, Mark, ed. *The World Almanac.* New York: Pharos Books; annual.

In Context. Context Institute, PO Box 11470, Bainbridge Island, WA 98110; quarterly. See "Facts Out of Context."

Jackson, Robert, ed. *Global Issues.* Guilford, CT: Dushkin Publishing Group; annual. Dushkin also publishes annuals on *Africa, Canadian Politics, China, World Politics, Comparative Politics, Environment, Geography, Latin America, Middle East and the Islamic World, Eastern Europe, Western Civilization, Western Europe, World History,* and *World Politics.*

Judson, S., ed. *A Manual on Non-violence and Children.* Philadelphia: New Society Publishers, 1984.

Kidron, Michael, and Ronald Segal. *The New State of the World Atlas.* New York: Simon and Schuster, 1987.

Krupp, Robin Rector. *Let's Go Traveling.* New York: William Morrow, 1992.

Lankford, Mary. *Hopscotch around the World.* New York: William Morrow, 1992.

Lombardi, Cathryn, and John Lombardi. *Latin American History: A Teaching Atlas.* Madison: University of Wisconsin Press, 1983.

One World: Countries Database. Culver City, CA: Social Studies School Service, 1985.

Opposing Viewpoints. St. Paul: Greenhaven Press. A series of books, each with a particular topic, containing a variety of articles arguing opposing viewpoints. Titles include *Central America, China, The Environmental Crisis, Immigration, Japan, Problems of Africa, The Political Spectrum, The Third World, War and Human Nature.*

Orlick, T. *The Co-operative Sports and Games Book.* New York: Writers and Readers Publishing, 1982.

Polon, Linda, and Aileen Cantwell. *The Whole Earth Holiday Book.* Glenview, IL: Scott, Foresman, 1983.

Reese, Lyn, and Jean Wilkinson. *Women in the World: Annotated History Resources for the Secondary Student.* Metuchen, NJ: Scarecrow Press, 1987.

Schniedewind, N., and E. Davidson. *Open Minds to Equality: A Sourcebook of Learning Activities to Promote Race, Sex, Class, and Age Equity.* Englewood Cliffs, NJ: Prentice-Hall, 1983.

Seager, Joni. *The State of the Earth Atlas.* New York: Simon and Schuster, 1990.

Sivard, Ruth Leger. *Women...A World Survey.* Washington, DC: World Priorities, 1985.

_____ *World Military and Social Expenditures.* Washington, DC: World Priorities; annual.

Williams, Sonja. *Exploding the Hunger Myths.* San Francisco: Institute for Food and Development Policy, 1987.

Women in World Culture Series. Originally published by GEM Publications, the series is now published by Glenhurst Publications, Central Community Center, 6300 Walker St., Saint Louis Park, MN. The series includes studies of women in Africa, Islam, Israel, Latin America, Modern China, Traditional China, and the former USSR.

World Bank Atlas, The. Washington, DC: World Bank, 1991.

World History Slide Collection, The (non-European history). Instructional Resources Corporation, Annapolis, MD, 1988. 2400 slides of non-European history categorized by region and time period, contains a Master Guide explaining each slide. A European history is also available. Order from Instructional Resources Corporation, 1819 Bay Ridge Ave., Annapolis, MD 21403; 800-922-1711.

World Population Data Sheet. Washington, DC: Population Reference Bureau; published each May.

World Press Review. Stanley Foundation, 200 Madison Ave., New York, NY; monthly.

Wright, John, ed. *The Universal Almanac.* Kansas City: Andrews and McMeel; annual.

Global Education Organizations and Curriculum Development Centers

The American Forum for Global Education
45 John St., Suite 908
New York, NY 10038

Materials on wide range of global education topics. The publication *Intercom* is quite useful.

The Asia Society
Education and Communications Department
725 Park Ave.
New York, NY 10021

Materials for educators interested in learning and teaching about Asian societies and cultures.

Center for Public Education in International Affairs,
School of International Relations (CPE)
VKC 328
University of Southern California
Los Angeles, CA 90089-0043

A national teacher education and curriculum development center in international and intercultural studies.

Center for Teaching International Relations (CTIR)
Graduate School of International Relations
University of Denver
Denver, CO 80208

A graduate center for research and training in global awareness education. One of the most comprehensive resource centers for global education materials for K-16.

Choices Education Project
Center for Foreign Policy Development
Brown University
Box 1948
Providence, RI 02912

Develops and publishes kits for analysis and discussion of significant foreign policy issues. Especially good for high school and college.

Constitutional Rights Foundation
601 South Kingsley
Los Angeles, CA 90005

A nonpartisan pioneer in the fields of law-related and citizenship education, with materials focusing on international legal issues.

Council on Interracial Books for Children
1842 Broadway, Suite 608
New York, NY 10032

Send for catalogue on books and materials.

Educational Resources, Inc.
7219 Blair Road, N.W.
Washington, DC 20012

Publishes *Your World: An International Paper for Young People.* This includes a Teacher/Parent Discussion Guide.

Educators for Social Responsibility
23 Garden St.
Cambridge, MA 02138

Produces and distributes peace education curricula and resource guides.

Foreign Policy Association
729 7th Ave.
New York, NY 10019

Focuses on study and development of materials for major foreign policy issues. Publishes *Great Decisions,* which is useful for high school and university students.

Global Alliance for Transforming Education (GATE)
4202 Ashwoody Trail
Atlanta, GA 30319

A relatively young organization concerned with holistic and alternative education.

Global Education Associates
475 Riverside Dr., Suite 456
New York, NY 10115

Publishes *Global Education Resource Guide.*

Global Graphics and Resources
2108 Hillside Dr.
Burlingame, CA 94010

Maps, flags, books, games, puzzles, globes, and posters.

Global Resource Center
6300 Walker St.
Saint Louis Park, MN 55416

Lots of good advice and resources on printed and video material on women globally.

Intercultural Press, Inc.
PO Box 700
Yarmouth, ME 04096

Catalogue of multicultural and cross-cultural classroom and training materials.

Moorehead Kennedy Institute
45 John Street, Suite 908
New York, NY 10038

An excellent source of simulations for colleges, universities, and junior and senior high schools.

People to People International
501 East Armour Blvd.
Kansas City, MO 64109

Arranges pen pal relationships between schools in the United States and other countries.

Piñata Publications
PO Box 10587
Oakland, CA 94610-0587

Publication materials include calendars on African Americans, Asian Americans, Native Americans, Folk Tales, Holidays, Sign Language, and other subjects.

Population Reference Bureau (PRB)
Population Education Programs
1875 Connecticut Ave., N.W., Suite 520
Washington, DC 20009

PRB has developed a number of learning packages dealing with population issues, as well as their various data sheets. Of particular note is "Teenage Parents: A Global Perspective." This comes with a teacher's guide and is appropriate for middle and high schools.

REACH Center
239 North McLeod
Arlington, WA 98223

REACH stands for Respecting Ethnic and Cultural Heritage and includes REACH for Kids, Project REACH and the Global REACH Consortium.

Social Studies School Service
10200 Jefferson Blvd.
PO Box 802
Culver City, CA 90232

A clearinghouse for educational materials. Check for a game called Bafá Bafá. This is one of the best cross-cultural simulations. It is a powerful educational experience which requires two class periods (at least) and two rooms, but is worth the trouble.

Stanford Program on International and
Cross-Cultural Education (SPICE)
Littlefield Center
Stanford University
Stanford, CA 94305

An excellent source of materials on China, Japan, Africa, Eastern Europe, and Latin America with some materials on nuclear arms and arms control. Many of the units include a packet of slides as well as background and discussion materials and bibliography.

Stanley Foundation
216 Sycamore, Suite 500
Muscatine, IA 52761

A collection of resources built over two decades and a staff who can consult and share experiences.

United Nations Publications Catalogue Sales Section
Room DC2-853, Department 701
New York, NY 10017

Contains reference sources, including studies, reports, yearbooks, official records, and periodicals.

U.S. Committee for UNICEF
Education Department
Information Center on Children's Cultures
333 East 38th St.
New York, NY 10016

A free catalogue and lots of educational materials, including slides, health kits, booklets, posters, and videos.

Women's History Center
6300 Walker St.
Saint Louis Park, MN 55416

Women in World Area Studies program develops curriculum units for secondary students on the contemporary interests and contributions of women in developing countries.

World Eagle, Inc.
64 Washburn Ave.
Wellesley, MA 02181

Publishes current, comparative data, graphs, and maps on a variety of topics reflecting social, political, and economic aspects of the United States and the world.

About the Authors

Jan Drum is founder and program director of Rediscovering fire, a newly-formed, nonprofit organization which offers innovative programs for people who want to rediscover the fire in their lives and lend energy to healing the planet. In 1991 she left the position of vice president of the Stanley Foundation, Muscatine, Iowa, where for 17 years she designed and coordinated global education and leadership development programs. Jan has led scores of workshops, conferences, and seminars for both young people and adults and has written extensively about her work in monographs, articles, and the monthly publication *Teachable Moments*.

Dr. Steven Hughes is a professor of political science at California State University, Stanislaus. He also serves as codirector of the Program in International and Multicultural Education which assists elementary and high school teachers in "internationalizing" curriculum. Steve is former chairman of the board of Las Palomas de Taos, a non-profit organization which offers a variety of educational programs in Taos, New Mexico.

George Otero is the founder and chairman of the board of Las Palomas de Taos, a nonprofit educational center devoted to empowering and assisting individuals and groups to actively and positively meet the challenges of our changing and diverse world. Dr. Otero has authored hundreds of activities on global themes. He has conducted scores of global education training programs nationwide and has worked closely with schools and organizations as they seek to include global issues in their curriculum. For the past three years, through a grant from the Mott Foundation of Flint, Michigan, Dr. Otero has been developing global education materials especially for community educators. He centers his work in Taos, New Mexico, at the historic Mable Dodge Luhan House.